Peter Henderson

Garden and Farm Topics

Peter Henderson

Garden and Farm Topics

ISBN/EAN: 9783337068929

Printed in Europe, USA, Canada, Australia, Japan

Cover: Foto ©Lupo / pixelio.de

More available books at **www.hansebooks.com**

GARDEN

AND

FARM TOPICS.

PETER HENDERSON,

AUTHOR OF

"*Gardening for Profit,*" "*Practical Floriculture,*" "*Gardening for Pleasure,*" and "*Hand-Book of Plants.*"

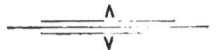

NEW YORK:
PUBLISHED BY PETER HENDERSON & CO.,
35 & 37 CORTLANDT STREET.

1884.

Entered, according to Act of Congress, in the year 1884, by
PETER HENDERSON & CO.,
In the office of the Librarian of Congress, Washington, D. C.

PRINTED BY E. S. DODGE, 95 CHAMBERS STREET, NEW YORK.

CONTENTS.

	PAGE.
Popular Bulbs and their Culture,	9
The Hyacinth, (*Hyacinthus*,)	9
The Tulip, (*Tulipa*,)	13
The Lily, (*Lilium*,)	18
The Lily of the Valley, (*Convallaria*,)	23
The Narcissus, (*Narcissus*,)	25
The Gladiolus, (*Gladiolus*,)	27
The Tuberose, (*Polianthes tuberosa*,)	32
The Calla, Egyptian Lily, Lily of the Nile, (*Richardia*,)	37
The Amaryllis, (*Amaryllis*,)	39
The Crocus, (*Crocus*,)	41
The Iris, (*Iris*,)	42
The Cyclamen, (*Cyclamen*,)	43
The Ranunculus, (*Ranunculus*),	45
The Wind Flower, (*Anemone*,)	46
The Crown Imperial, Fritillary, (*Fritillaria*.)	47
The Snow-drop, (*Galanthus*,)	47
The Tropæolum, (*Nasturtium*,)	48
The Arum, (*Arum*,)	50
The Ixia, (*Ixia*,)	51
The Guernsey Lily, (*Nerine*,)	51
The Sparaxis, (*Sparaxis*,)	52
The Babiana, (*Babiana*,)	53
The Amazon Lily, (*Eucharis*,)	53
The Oxalis, (*Oxalis*,)	54
Squills, Scillas, (*Scilla*,)	56
Window Gardening, Basket Plants, and Care of Plants in Rooms,	57
Propagation of Plants by Cuttings, Layers, Division, and Seed,	67

	PAGE.
Rose Growing in Winter,	87
Green-house Structures and Modes of Heating,	99
Formation and Renovation of Lawns,	117
Onoin Growing for Market,	123
How to Grow Cabbage and Cauliflower, (Early and Late,)	137
Growing and Preserving of Celery for Winter,	159
Strawberry Culture,	169
Root Crops for Farm Stock,	177
Culture of Alfalfa or Lucerne, (*Medicago sativa*,)	187
Manures and their Modes of Application,	193
Market Gardening around New York,	201
The Use of the Feet in Sowing and Planting,	211
Popular Errors and Scientific Dogmas,	219
Humbugs in Horticulture,	227
Draining,	241

INTRODUCTION.

THE demand for special information in a condensed form, on most of the subjects embraced in this work, by hundreds of our patrons each season, is the chief reason for its publication. For example, an inexperienced grower of *Cabbages, Celery,* or *Onions,* wishes for information about methods of getting the best crops; another is about to form a *Strawberry bed,* a *lawn,* or *construct a green-house,* and he asks the benefit of my veteran experience. No reply by letter on such subjects can be very satisfactory, and hence the necessity of brief printed instructions, which, I trust, have been as clearly given as the limited space would admit.

Such, however, as require a more elaborate treatise on the general subject I beg to refer, if full information is wanted for *Market Gardening,* to my book, "GARDENING FOR PROFIT;" if for *Commercial Floriculture,* to "PRACTICAL FLORICULTURE;" if for reference to *Nomenclature and History and Description of Plants,* to the "HAND-BOOK OF PLANTS;" and if for *General Gardening for Amateurs,* to "GARDENING FOR PLEASURE."

PETER HENDERSON.

JERSEY CITY HEIGHTS, N. J.,
Jan. 1, 1884.

GARDEN

—AND—

FARM TOPICS.

POPULAR BULBS AND THEIR CULTURE.

THE HYACINTH, (Hyacinthus.)

THE Hyacinth is placed first in the list of bulbs, as it certainly deserves to be. Its easy culture, both in-doors and out; its immense variety of double and single flowers, embracing nearly every shade of color; and its delicious fragrance, all combine to make it pre-eminent above all other bulbs, if not above all other families of plants, the Rose excepted. It was first introduced into England in 1596. Gerarde, in his "Herbal," published near the end of the sixteenth century, describes four kinds, the single and the double blue, the purple, and the violet; and John Parkinson, writing in 1629, describes eight kinds, among which, by this time, white and red colors had appeared.

During the two and a half centuries that have passed since Parkinson wrote, there has been a steady improvement in the size, form, and color of the flowers of this plant. From the eight varieties of 1629, described by John Parkinson, more than four thousand varieties have been produced and catalogued, from which number upward of two hundred varieties are subjects of extensive commerce. The Hyacinth is a universal favorite in the most extended application of the word. The number of its varieties is now fully equal to that of any other florist's flower. They are largely grown for forcing into flower in the dull, cheerless months of winter and early spring, when their delicately-colored flowers and rich fragrance lend a charm to be found in nothing else.

FORCING.

For forcing, the bulbs should be potted about the middle of September in five or six inch pots in rich, light earth, and placed in a cold frame or under a wall, where they can be covered with wooden shutters, or some similar contrivance, to keep off heavy rains. In either case they should be covered a foot thick with hay or leaves ; and being once well watered after potting, they may be left for a month to form their roots, when the most forward should be brought out, and after re-potting into larger pots, according to the apparent strength of the bulbs, should be placed in a temperature of about 50°. Some care is necessary in the application and increase of heat, or the flowers will be abortive. It should not exceed 50° for the first three weeks, but afterward may be increased gradually to 60° or 65°; and if the pots are plunged into bottom heat the same careful increase should be observed, or the points of the roots will infallibly be killed. One-third the depth of the pot is fully sufficient at first, and if the heat is brisk they should not be plunged more than half way at any time. When the flower stems have risen to nearly their full height, and the lower flowers of the spike are beginning to expand, the plants should be removed to a lower temperature, usually afforded by the green-house; and when the flowers are fully expanded, the plants can be taken to the sitting-room, or wherever their presence is desired, observing to protect them from sudden changes or cold draughts of air, and it will help them if the water given to them should be moderately warm, say from 80° to 100°.

Growing in Glasses.

Hyacinths in glasses are an elegant and appropriate ornament to the parlor, and for this purpose occasion little trouble. The bulbs should be procured and placed in the glasses as early in the season as possible, keeping them in the dark until their roots are well started, after which the lightest position that can be afforded is the best. The water in which they grow should be changed twice or thrice a week, and in severe weather the plants must be removed from the window, so as to be secure from frost.

Out-door Culture.

For decorating the flower garden, the bulbs should be planted in October or the early part of November, at six or seven inches apart each way, in light, rich soil, at a depth of four inches from the crown of the bulb to the surface of the earth, and covered over, as soon as the ground freezes, with three or four inches of leaves or rough manure. It may be necessary to place sticks to them when in bloom, to prevent them from being broken by the wind; and this is all the attention they require till the foliage is withered, and the season has arrived for taking them up, when, instead of the usual practice of drying them at once in the sun, we would advise the Dutch method to be adopted, namely, to place them side by side on a sunny spot of ground, and cover them with about an inch of loose earth, to thoroughly ripen by the subdued heat imparted to the earth which surrounds them. Left in this position for a fortnight, they will become dry and firm, and an hour or two of sunshine will finish them properly for storing. So treated, they will be but little inferior to imported bulbs.

The multiplication and growth of Hyacinths for sale is principally carried on out of doors in the vicinity of Haarlem, in Holland. The sandy soil, and moisture of both soil and climate in that country, are peculiarly favorable to the growth of the Hyacinth. Hundreds of acres are there devoted to the culture of these and kindred plants, and the Haarlem gardens are a gay sight from the early season of the year till far on in the summer. The process of multiplication is carried on by sowing the seeds or by taking offsets from the parent bulb. By seeds new varieties only are obtained; it is by offsets that the already known and valued kinds are increased. The bulbs are cut crosswise, and sprinkled with sand to absorb any superfluous moisture that may exude from the incisions. After a time they are planted in the earth, when numerous small bulbs are formed on the edges of these incisions. At the expiration of one season they are again lifted from the ground, and the numerous small bulbs, still only partially developed, are separated from the parent root and planted out *again* and *again*, year after year, for three or four years, before they become flowering bulbs of fine market quality.

WHITE ROMAN HYACINTH.

The white Roman Hyacinth is largely used for forcing for winter flowers by the florists of New York and all large cities. In New York alone upward of five hundred thousand bulbs are used during the winter, and the number is rapidly increasing each year. The flower spikes average four cents each at wholesale. By a succession of plantings in boxes six inches deep, beginning in September, they are had in flower from November till May, and even later. The method pursued is similar to that for the Lily of the Valley. (See Lily of the Valley, (*Convallaria,*) where the method is described.)

THE TULIP, (Tulipa.)

TULIPS are divided into several classes, and of these we shall speak in the order of their flowering. . The single and double varieties of the *Duc van Thol*, of which the type is *Tulipa suaveolens*, (from the Latin *suavis*, sweet,) are the earliest and most suitable for pot culture or forcing. If, in autumn, they are planted singly in four-inch pots of light, rich soil, they will flower extremely well in an ordinary room, and contrast finely with Hyacinths in glasses. The culture is the same as for Hyacinths. They will flower in water like the Hyacinth, but with less certainty and less luxuriance; hence they are better grown in pots of soil. The *Duc van Thol* was introduced into English gardens from the South of Europe in 1603.

The Single Early Tulip, (*Tulipa Gesneriana,*) the parent of our ordinary garden varieties, is a native of Asia Minor, the Caucasus, Calabria, and Central Italy. Conrad Gesner, a Swiss naturalist, in whose honor it was named, first made it known by a description and drawing in April, 1559. Of this class of Early Single Tulips there is almost an endless variety. They have received, for more than two hundred years, all the care and attention that could possibly be bestowed on a plant, not only by the Dutch florists, but by nearly every skilled gardener throughout the Old World.

Notwithstanding the "mania" has safely passed over, one of the Haarlem florists this season (1883) offered two thousand varieties. To select from a list so large with a view of pleasing, or of securing the most desirable, would be to play a game of chance. Nearly every color and shade, except black, is represented, either alone or mixed, striped or shaded; in fact, every possible combination of color may be obtained. Double Tulips are almost as common as the single, many of them very showy and desirable. But, like all others who have made a specialty of the Tulip, we could never admire the double as much as the single varieties. Late flowering or Show Tulips have been grown from seed by millions, the result of which has been the acquisition of many superb varieties.

There is a singularity in Tulips which belongs to no other flower. The seedlings generally, when they first bloom, produce flowers without any stripes or markings, but with a yellow base, the upright portion of the petals being self-colored, brown, red, purple, scarlet, or rose. In this state, when they have been grown for years without variation, they are called Breeders or Mother Tulips. These are planted every year until they break into stripes, when, if the markings are fine, or different from any known, they are named. Each person who has "broken" one claims and has a perfect right to give it a name; but much confusion naturally exists, because of the fact that different names have been given to those that have broken almost exactly alike. In a bed of a thousand seedlings, it is not probable that any two will be very nearly alike in their markings, and none are ever identically the same. This uncertainty adds greatly to the charm of Tulip cultivation. The hope of something new in the markings and penciling is a sufficient stimulus for the enthusiast to persevere in his labor until he has found *one* worthy of a name. A singular feature in the Tulip is, that after it breaks it ever remains the same.

Show Tulips are divided into three classes: 1. *Byblæmens*, such as have a white ground, variegated with purple, the edges well feathered, the leaflets erect, and the whole forming a perfect cup. 2. *Bizarres*, having a yellow ground, variegated with scarlet, purple, rose, or violet. 3. *Roses*, with white ground, variegated with rose-color, scarlet, or crimson. The properties of a good Tulip as a florist's flower, according to the London Horticultural Society's rules, are, " 1. The cup should form, when quite expanded, from half to a third of a round ball. To do this, the petals must be six in number, broad at the ends, smooth at the edges, and the divisions between the petals must scarcely show any indenture. 2. The three inner petals should set closely to the three outer ones, and the whole should be broad enough to allow of the fullest expansion without quartering, as it is called, or exhibiting any vacancy between the petals. 3. The petals should be thick, smooth, and stiff, and keep their form well. 4. The ground should be clear and distinct, whether white or yellow. The least stain, even at the lower end of the petal, renders a Tulip of less value. 5. Whatever be the disposition of colors or marks upon a Tulip, all the six petals should be marked alike, and be, therefore, perfectly uniform. 6. The feathered flowers should have an even, close feathering all round; and whether narrow or wide, light or heavy, should reach far enough round the petals to form, when expanded, an unbroken edging. 7. If the flower have any marking besides the feathering at the edge, it should be a bold mark down the center, but not reaching the bottom of the cup. The mark must be similar in all the six petals. 8. Flowers not feathered, and with the flame only, must have no marks on the edges of the flowers. None of the colors must break through to the edge. The color may be disposed in any form, so that it be perfectly uniform in all the petals, and does not go too near the bottom. 9. The color, whatever it may be, must be dense and decided. Whether it be delicate and light, or bright, or dark, it must be distinct in its outline, and not shaded, or flushed, or broken. 10. The height should be eighteen to thirty-six inches; the former is right for the outside row in a bed, and the latter is right for the highest row. 11. The purity of the white and the brightness of the yellow should be permanent; that is to say, should stand until the petals actually fall." Parrot Tulips are ignored by those florists who claim the right to say what is and what is not beautiful. Not being bound to observe the "laws" that regulate the form, shape, and "perfect markings," we prize this class very highly, on account of their singularly picturesque appearance. The flowers are very large, and the colors exceedingly brilliant. They are unequaled for groups in mixed borders, or conspicuous places in front of shrubs. The varieties of this class are limited, but they are, nevertheless, particularly beautiful.

SOIL AND CULTURE.

The best soil for the culture of the Tulip is a rich, rather light, well-drained loam. A bed of sufficient size for planting the bulbs should be dug at least twelve inches deep. The bulbs should then be planted six inches apart each way; pressed deep enough to keep them in their places, and covered with mould to the depth of three inches on the sides of the bed, and five inches in the center. This precaution is necessary, that water may not stand on the bed during the winter. When the bed is planted and covered, it may be left to the weather until the Tulips come up, or about the first of March. A slight protection of litter is then required, as the frost has a tendency to check the bloom. When the flowers appear, if they are protected from the sun by a light canvas, the period of bloom may be kept up for three or four weeks. The colors are generally better if not shaded at all, but in that case the bloom would be soon over. Sometimes a single day's hot sun will completely spoil them.

When the flowers begin to fade, they should be cut away and removed from the bed. As soon as the stems of the Tulip turn yellow, and the leaves begin to dry they may be taken up and put in a cool, dry place. When dry, thoroughly clean off the old skin and dirt, and put in paper bags, ready for planting out again in October. The Tulip is also now extensively forced for cut flowers during the winter and spring months. The method of culture is identical with that of the Roman Hyacinth and Paper Narcissus, which see.

THE LILY, (Lilium.)

Out-door Culture.

This genus, the type of an extensive order, numbers upward of sixty species, and is eminently distinguished for its surpassing loveliness, and its rare combination of grandeur and chaste beauty. A remarkable feature in this family of plants is, that it has no *poor relations*. In a general collection of the species, all that can be imagined desirable and perfect in floral forms will be realized. A great inducement to the cultivation of this genus is their ease of culture, and their almost perfect hardiness, thriving with all the vigor of indigenous forms when planted in the flower border. All of them delight in light, rich soil, such as is afforded by a mixture of loam and well-rotted manure, and one uniform treatment is applicable under all circumstances to the whole of the species ; all may be grown together in the border, and remain undisturbed a number of years, frequent removals being injurious, by destroying the roots. All the species thrive best when planted in partial shade, the shrubbery border, or in large beds in an open grove. They are propagated by offsets or by scales.

When the old bulbs have several small ones formed around them, take them up in October, divide them into single bulbs, and replant the large flowering bulbs immediately in fresh, rich earth, where they are to flower. Plant the small bulbs in a bed of the same kind of soil by themselves ; let them remain until sufficiently large and strong for flowering, which should require but two years; then take them up, select the larger bulbs, and plant them where they are to remain, taking care to enrich the earth with well decomposed manure, the small ones to be replanted as before. *L. candidum*, "Easter Lily," should be taken up and replanted in August or first part of September, as the bulbs make a growth in autumn, upon which in a great measure depends their flowering the coming season. In selecting the situation for the Lily-bed, care should be taken to have the dryest spot

LILIUM AURATUM.

possible, where water is not liable to stand in the winter. A good mulching of leaves, coarse manure, or evergreen boughs will prove highly beneficial.

The species are pretty generally distributed throughout the temperate regions of the northern hemisphere; a few only are found in the mountains of sub-tropical Asia. California has furnished several that are among the more difficult to cultivate here, because of the difference in the seasons of growth. Japan has furnished by far the greater number of really excellent species, among which are *L. auratum*, or Golden Banded; *L. speciosum* and its varieties ; *L. Kramerii, L. Leichtlinii, L. tigrinum flora plena, L. Thunbergianum* in variety, *L. longiflorum*. *L. candidum*, the oldest known species, comes from the Levant. Asia furnishes *L. Chalcedonicum ;* Siberia the beautiful little *L. tenuifolium*, which is there grown as an article of food. The United States contributes *L. superbum*, *L. Canadense*, *L. Philadelphicum*, *L. Catesbæi*, *L. Carolinianum*, and *L. Columbianum*, together with *L. Washingtonianum*, *L. Humboldtii*, *L. parvum*, *L. Californicum*, *L. pardalinum*, *L. Roezlii*, *L. Parryi*, and *L. Walkerii*, from California. It may be added here that the California Lilies often remain in the ground a whole year before growing.

FORCING.

All the varieties succeed well grown in pots; but two, *L. candidum* and *L. longiflorum*, bear what is termed *forcing*, or are made to bloom out of their natural season. The *L. speciosum* class and *L. auratum* do not force well. *L. candidum*, or the white panicled Easter Lily, is the species so extensively forced for flowers for Easter. The method is to plant the bulbs in six-inch pots, deep enough to merely cover the bulb, any time from September 1st to December 1st, plunging the pots of those potted early to the rims out of doors in a sheltered, warm spot, and covering up with leaves as cold weather approaches, so that they shall not get frozen at any time. Those that are potted later, say from the middle of November, should be plunged in the same way either in the soil under the benches in a cold green-house or in a cold frame. The object is in all cases to get them to fill the pot with roots in a low temperature. When the pots are well filled with roots, they may be brought into a higher temperature, say 55° at night and 10° or 15° higher in the daytime. If the pots are well filled with roots they will come into flower from eight to ten weeks after being placed in the above temperature. When the flower stems begin to ascend, the plants may be liberally supplied with liquid manure (made from one bushel of

LILIUM HARRISII.

THE BERMUDA LILY.

cow manure to fifty gallons of water) once a week or so, taking care, however, never to water unless the plant shows indications of being dry.

The treatment given above for *L. candidum* will also answer for *L. longiflorum*, the white Trumpet Lily, except that the latter should first be put in four-inch pots, and remain until well filled with roots, or until the plant is three to four inches high; then shift into a six-inch, placing the ball on the bottom, so that all, or nearly all, the fresh mould is at the top. When the second pot is well filled with roots, shift as before into a seven-inch pot pot, where they can remain until they come into flower. Soon after flowering this variety will show a disposition to rest, and if allowed but a short period, and repotted into an eight-inch pot without disturbing the roots, and kept in a cool house, they will again come into flower in September and October. Again, after a short rest, they will, without a change, make a new growth and flower in the following spring, by which time the bulbs will have become so exhausted as to need planting in the border for at least two years. A new variety of *L. longiflorum*, known as *L. Harrisii*, has larger flowers and is more abundant in flowering. The treatment is the same as for the older sort. These Lilies may also be forced by placing the bulbs at once in the pots in which they are intended to flower. Large numbers of them are forced for Easter.

LILY OF THE VALLEY, (Convallaria.)

THE Lily of the Valley, *Convallaria majalis*, is a plant so well known, and such a universal favorite, that little need be said by way of description, unless we add that of Gerarde in 1596, which is as follows: "The Lilly of the Vally hath many leaves like the smallest leaves of Water Plantaine, among which riseth vp a naked stalke, halfe a foot high, garnished with many white floures, like bels, with blunt and turned edges, of a strong savour, yet pleasant enoughf, which being past, there come small, red berries, much like the berries of asparagus, wherein the seed is contained." A modern writer in the "Treasury of Botany" says: "Without poetical or fanciful conventionalities, the Lily of the Valley is as perfect an emblem of purity, modesty, and humility as the floral world can afford. It may seem idle to observe that a flower of this description cannot be that referred to in the Sermon on the Mount; but as that opinion is frequently broached in popular works, it may simply be observed that it never grows in the open field, and that there is nothing in its array to which the term 'glory' is applicable. Not a litlte unprofitable commentary might have been spared if

LILY OF THE VALLEY. (*Convallaria Majalis.*)

the same general meaning had been attached to the term 'Lilies of the Field' which has, by common consent, been ascribed to the parallel phrase 'Fowls of the Air,' while the passage itself would have gained in force and dignity by being kept clear from botanical disquisitions."

The flowers of the Lily of the Valley are used during the winter months in immense quantities, New York city alone probably using a million, the average price of which is about five cents each, so that for this flower alone $50,000 are annually paid by the bouquet makers to the florist, the consumer paying, no doubt, one-third more. The Lily of the Valley is nearly all imported from Germany and France, usually in single crowns or "pips."

FORCING.

The method of culture is to place these very thickly together in shallow boxes, as soon as received in November, placing them in a cold frame, or in the open ground, covering them up so that they do not get frozen. It is a popular belief that they are benefited by being frozen; but this is a mistake. They must be kept at the low temperature to be found usually in a cold frame or when covered up in the open ground, which is usually from 35° to 40°; but they gain no advantage by being even slightly frozen, and may be seriously hurt by severe freezing. They should remain in this condition at least four weeks before they are brought in to force, which should be done gradually, beginning at 50° and running up to 65° or 70°. If taken in every few weeks, a succession may be kept up from January until May. In fact, the flowers are now to be had all the year round, as some growers find it sufficiently profitable to keep the roots in refrigerators, and, thus retarded, they are forced to bloom at will at any time during the summer or fall months. This same system might be used with many other bulbs, such as the Tuberose or Hyacinth, but it is only in very valuable flowers, such as the Lily of the Valley, that the expense would be justified. The plant does well in the garden, and may be put under the shade of trees ; but wherever placed, the roots should not be disturbed for several years, if at all, as many clumps will not otherwise bloom. It is useless to save the Lily of the Valley roots after having been forced. It is better to throw them away, as it takes years for them to recuperate.

THE NARCISSUS, (Narcissus).

IN this genus we have a long list of established favorites, remarkable alike for the elegance, fragrance, and earliness of their flowers. In one respect the species are all alike : they delight in rich soil made porous with plenty of sand and well-rotted manure. All of them are also quite hardy, and from the early period at which their flowers are produced, they are of the utmost consequence to the flower gardener.

FORCING.

Several of the species are found to bear forcing well, and for this purpose have become a staple article in the Dutch florists' trade, and several varieties have been originated by them, suited, by the selection of their parentage, to bear this trying course of treatment. The following are commonly grown for forcing : *Bazelman Major*, *Soleil d'Or*, *Grande Primo*, and *Grande Monarque*. These, with the double Roman and others, should be potted in September in a mixture of equal parts of fresh loam, rotted manure, and leaf mould, with half of either quantity of sand. In potting, the neck of the bulb should be kept above the surface of the soil, that the roots may have so much more space in the pot ; and when the potting is completed they should be placed together, either in a cold frame or in some convenient place, so that they may be covered a foot thick with fresh leaves. These exclude light and prevent frost from getting to the roots, both essential to a speedy excitement of root-growth.

In about five or six weeks it will be found that many of them have filled the pots with roots, and these may be taken into a temperature of 55° to bring on their flowers ; and if re-potted when the first two leaves have grown a few inches, the flowers will be considerably larger ; but before any plant is taken from the bed of leaves, be sure that it has made a good stock of healthy roots, or it will be spoiled by the forcing process. Narcissi do not require a powerful heat to bring out their flowers, (55° will do it better than any other,) and the supply of water should be sufficient, but by no means excessive.

The Paper Narcissus, *N. papyraceus*, is now, perhaps, more extensively forced than either of the above mentioned. It is grown in immense quantities by the florists of New York and other large cities, and, next to the Roman Hyacinth, is the bulb most extensively grown for this purpose. When grown on a large scale it is planted in boxes of soil about five inches deep, at a distance of three to four inches apart, and treated as recommended above. This, like nearly all other bulbs, is of no value after being forced, and the roots may be thrown away.

When grown in the open borders the bulbs should be planted in October, in newly dug and well-manured ground, at a depth of three inches, reckoning from the top of the bulb to the surface of the soil. This will not be too much for any, except, perhaps, the Jonquils, which, from having smaller bulbs, may be placed an inch nearer the top. At this depth, and with plenty of manure about them, water will not be required, but they will grow strong and flower finely. When planted in beds, and it becomes necessary to remove them to make room for other plants, it should be done as soon as their beauty is past. As the bulbs are by no means mature at this time, they should be "laid in" in some slightly shaded place until the foliage is quite withered, when they may be taken up, dried, and stored away until wanted for the next planting season.

Most of the species are from the south of Europe, and are propagated by offsets. They were among the earliest cultivated garden flowers.

THE GLADIOLUS, (Gladiolus.)

This extensive and well-known genus consists of upward of sixty species. With but few exceptions, which will be noted in their descriptions, they are natives of the Cape of Good Hope. They are remarkable for ease of culture, grace of habit, and for the beauty and intense coloring of the flowers, which varies from the most brilliant scarlet to pure white, from clear rose to pure yellow and bright purple. The habits of the species are as varied as their colors; some delicate and light, others strong and robust, with constitutions adapted to any climate excepting the most frigid. From these species some of the most remarkable hybrids have been produced. In no branch of floriculture has the skill, the zeal, and the perseverance of the hybridizer been so liberally rewarded. A class with almost unlimited numbers of varieties has been produced, that, for the size of flower, beauty of form, size and strength of plant, together with the enormous length of flower spike, are entirely unknown to the species. So popular have these hybrids become that the species are only to be found in botanical collections.

HYBRID GLADIOLUS.

The hybridization of any popular tribe, particularly when it is attended with so little labor, in proportion to the results produced, as in this class, is speedily carried to an extent which renders characteristic distinctions indefinable; and perhaps the introduction of the numberless names which necessarily arise out of such a circumstance is to be regretted, as occasioning difficulty and labor beyond what most cultivators are disposed to submit to. For the purposes of sale, however, and also to enable the producer to recommend very particular sorts to dealers and amateurs, it is essential that every seedling or variety that is at all deserving of being perpetuated should have a distinctive name. The many hundred named garden varieties of Gladioli are descendants of *G. Gandavensis,* but how and where this variety was produced has been for a long time an open question; why, we could never fully understand, for we have the word of one of the most prominent horticulturists in the world, Louis Van Houtte, whose word was authority whenever given, that it was produced at Ghent, and was a cross between *G. psittacinus* and *G. cardinalis.* This we should consider a full settlement of the question; not so, however; for the late Hon. and Rev. William Herbert, an acknowledged authority on bulbs, says Mr. Van

Houtte is in error; for after repeated attempts to hybridize the two, he, Mr. Herbert, could not succeed; consequently it could not be done, and what Mr. Van Houtte said had been done was a mistake. All the English writers agree with Mr. Herbert, and say the origin of *G. Gandavensis* is obscure. There is no question, however, as to the fact, that to *G. Gandavensis* we are indebted for all our fine garden varieties, as it crosses freely with many of the species, and each cross seems to possess merits superior to either parent. It is a common mistake to call our many varieties hybrids, when in reality they are all, or nearly all, cross-breeds ; and this is one of the most interesting features in Gladioli culture, that every cross between well-known varieties tends in almost every case to improve, not only the beauty of the flower, but the vigor of the plant.

Raising from Seed.

We wish now to remove, as far as possible, the prevalent erroneous idea, that it is a difficult task to raise new and choice varieties from seed. The only secret, the only mystery is, that one can with so little trouble and expense produce flowers that will give such intense satisfaction and pleasure. It is no more trouble to raise Gladioli from seed than it is to raise the most common vegetable. With the simplest garden culture, there is an almost absolute certainty of success. Prepare your bed in spring as for any hardy annual, sow your seed, and cover to the depth of one inch. Hoe as often as needed for other crops ; keep them well weeded ; take up the bulbs after a frost, or before, if they show signs of ripening ; store them in a dry cellar, free from frost ; plant them out again the next spring, and the ensuing summer very many of them will flower. If the precaution is taken to sow the seed in a hot-bed, close the same upon the approach of a heavy rain, which they dislike exceedingly. Very nearly all the bulbs will be large enough to give their most perfect flowers the second year. The fact that the best rarely flower first, will tend to create in the amateur a warm and lively interest.

A pertinent question is, how to obtain the best seed. Commence by making a careful selection of the best varieties in cultivation, keeping in view those of the best form, largest size, and of the most intense and positive colors; wherever they are marked or variegated, have the markings bold and distinct. Plant all in a bed so that they will not be more than one foot apart each way. Without further care you will get some good seed; but a better quality and much larger quantity will be obtained by crossing them in all sorts of ways, which is the most effectually done on a dry day, when there is but little air stirring. It is not necessary to cross fertilize for good varieties, though it is a more certain way; yet very many of our best seedlings were accidentals; artificial fertilization being necessary from the fact of their rarely fertilizing themselves.

SOIL.

The Gladiolus dislikes a stiff, clayey soil, but will thrive well in almost any other, its preference being for one of a moist, sandy nature, or light loam. It does best on what is termed sod ground, with but little manure, and that well rotted. Successive plantings in the same ground should be avoided Change the locality of the bed every year, so as not to return to the same spot for at least three years. It is much the best plan to make your ground very rich this year, and put on some light crop ; then it will be in perfect order for your Gladiolus the next.

Increase by Bulblets.

Increase of desirable sorts is effected by the small bulbs or bulblets that form at the base of the new bulb, which are produced in greater or less quantities. Some varieties will have on an average a hundred in a year; others will produce scarcely any. The bulblets should be planted in spring, and given the same treatment as recommended for the seed. If planted in rich, light soil, and attention given to careful weeding and mulching with leaf mould, saw-dust, or any such non-conducting material, so as to prevent the sun's rays from drying and heating up the soil too much, nearly all of the young bulblets will flower the second year. They should be sown in drills about six inches wide, or the width of a common hoe, and the drills about one foot apart. The bulblets or seedlings should be sown thick enough to touch each other. In this way they will do better than if sown too thin, as then the soil between the plants would get heated and dried up.

Time to Plant.

During the winter, Gladiolus bulbs, whether large or small, should be kept in a dry, cool cellar. As the bulb is nearly hardy, plantings may be set out as soon as the ground is fit to work in spring; and even should the ground be frozen after, they will sustain no injury.

Bulbs set out during April will be usually at their best flowering in August, but "succession plantings" may be made every ten days until the middle of July, which will give a succession of bloom the entire season. It is a common practice, with the New York florists, to reserve Gladiolus bulbs until August, which are then planted in boxes six or seven inches deep, in rich soil. The boxes are kept out-doors until frost, when they are placed in a cool green-house, where they flower in November, at a time when everything is done outside.

THE TUBEROSE, (Polianthes Tuberosa.)

THE original *Single* species is a native of the East Indies, and was introduced early in the sixteenth century. At a much more recent date the common or tall-growing *Double* Tuberose was raised from seed by Mons. Le Cour, of Leyden, Holland, who for many years would not part with a root, destroying all surplus, so that he could say that he had a monopoly of the only Double Tuberose in the world.

The recently introduced variety, known as the *Pearl*, is a sport, having originated on the grounds of Mr. John Henderson, of Flushing, L. I., in 1865. Its strong habit of growth, and dark, heavy foliage attracted Mr. Henderson's attention, causing him to give it every chance for perfect development. The result was a variety far superior to the parent, both in size and number of flowers, with a marked superiority in habit of growth, the flower-stalks not being so tall by nearly a foot as the original, a feature making it invaluable for green-house culture. I purchased the entire stock from Mr. Henderson, paying him about five hundred dollars for a barrel of the roots, and sold it for the first time in 1867.

The Tuberose delights in a strong, rich soil, deep and moist. Manure, heat, and water are essential to its perfect development. For cultivation in the open border, the bulbs should be planted about the first of June, covering the tuber about one inch with light, fine soil. No other care is needed than that usually given garden plants. The only care required is in the selection of the bulbs, which, if kept moist and cool during winter, are liable to rot away in the center, rendering them worthless for flowering. Perfect tubers will always be green at the top, or at least sufficiently so to show signs of life ; and in choosing, all others should be rejected.

Forcing.

Forcing the Tuberose, so as to have the flowers from January to March, is an exceedingly difficult operation, and is now but little attempted here. The plant being of tropical origin, to have it at all times in a growing state requires a high temperature—not less than an average of 80°; consequently, few ordinarily-heated greenhouses or private sitting-rooms are at a temperature high enough to insure the continued and uninterrupted growth necessary to the production of flowers in the dark winter months. It is, however, comparatively easily forced so as to produce flowers during April, May, and June, and again, by retarding the bulbs, during November and December. By the first method, the bulbs are, about the first of January, placed closely together in boxes three inches deep, having two inches or so of damp moss in the bottom. These boxes are placed in some warm spot, where the temperature will average 75°. If for greenhouse culture, the best place is on the hot-water pipes. In about four or five weeks the Tuberoses will have rooted all through the moss, and they should then be potted in four or five inch pots, or planted in a bench of soil four or five inches deep, and kept in a temperature at no time less than 75°, and flowers will be had in abundance in April. For succession crops, place the dry bulbs in moss, at intervals of three or four weeks. The last crops will usually be the best, as by May and June the temperature will have increased, and less artificial heat will be required.

If flowers are wanted during November and December, the retarding process alluded to is resorted to. This is done by selecting such bulbs as are wanted, (care being taken to use only such as are sound and firm,) and placing them in some cool, dry place until the middle of August, when the first crop may be planted, either in pots or in a bench of the green-house, as described above for the spring crop. This planting will produce a crop by November. For the succession crop for December, planting must be delayed until the middle of September, this being as late as the bulbs can be kept sound in the usual way; but they may be retarded in refrigerators, and in that way may be had all through the winter months, provided a high enough temperature, with plenty of light, can be given. The same high temperature is indispensable as in the spring crop, namely, an average of 75°. The variety best for forcing is the "Pearl," which grows only about half the height, and has flowers nearly twice the diameter of the old sort; but for planting in the open ground in the ordinary way, when the flowers are only wanted for fall, the common double variety is the best; as, being less full, the flowers open better under the often unfavorably dry atmosphere that we have in October.

Tuberoses are often forwarded, so as to be got in flower in the earlier fall months, in sections of the country where the season is too short. This is done exactly in the way recommended for the spring forcing, by

THE TUBEROSE.

starting the bulbs in damp moss; but for this purpose the dry bulbs should not be placed in the moss until the middle of May. By the middle of June, when the weather has become warm, and they are set out, they will start to grow at once, and will in this way flower from three to four weeks earlier than if the dry bulb had been put in the open ground, cold as it is in most of the Northern States in May. Of course, it will be understood, that when the dry bulbs are placed in the moss to start, it must be in a green-house, or in some place where the thermometer will average $75°$ or $80°$, or they will not start at all, or, at least, very feebly. It will thus be seen, from the foregoing remarks, that it will be utterly useless to attempt to grow Tuberoses at any season unless in a tropical temperature, which at no time should be less than $75°$, and if it *averages* $80°$, all the better.

Tendency to Sport.

Many growers of this flower have been sadly disappointed in the results, their flowers coming single instead of double, and they naturally ask the cause. We cán only say, there is a tendency in all sports and hybrids to return to the original or type, and this plant is no exception to the rule. The conditions of growth may have much to do with it. We have known large stocks that were wholly double one year to come nearly all single the next. We cannot satisfactorily account for it, and only know that the annoyance is common in every place where they are grown. From a very close observation, we believe much is due to poor cultivation, and the best remedy is to be found in giving them a very rich soil and good cultivation. Like many other plants, we have found they do best when given a rotation of soil.

FIELD CULTURE.

The field culture of Tuberose bulbs is now a large and important industry in this country, millions being grown, not only for home use, but for exportation to Europe. Hitherto they were grown almost exclusively in Italy, but within the past ten years European dealers in the bulb find they can buy a better article at a cheaper rate from us. We ourselves have for many years grown nearly half a million roots annually. Our plan of late years has been, after thoroughly plowing and harrowing, to mark out furrows, three and a half feet apart, with the plow (or, what is better, with the implement known as a furrow marker) six or seven inches deep and ten or twelve inches wide. In the bottom of this furrow is spread two or three inches of well-rotted stable manure, or bone dust thick enough to cover the soil. Two or three inches of soil are placed on the top of this, and the Tuberose sets are then planted in this prepared furrow in two rows nine or ten inches apart, and five or six inches between the sets. The object of this plan is, that we get the benefit of the manure for two rows instead of one, as is the case when one row only is planted in the furrow, in the usual way. It is a little more labor to cultivate, but the saving in manure, in time in making furrows, and in planting by the double row plan, we have found more than offsets this.

A great many Tuberoses are now grown in the Southern States; but, unless they are lifted and dried at the proper time, there is danger of the flower bud starting prematurely, which renders the bulb worthless. I had 20,000 sent from Florida a few years ago, that were perfectly worthless from this cause. They were left in the ground until November; probably two months too long, if the sets were large, and in consequence all had started an embryo flower bud in the dry bulb. It seems to me that the only safe way to grow good Tuberose bulbs in extreme Southern States is to use sets no larger than peas, if they are to be left in the ground till November. From such small sets there would be no danger of the flower bud forming prematurely. If larger sets are used, they should be lifted in September. When Tuberose bulbs are raised in Pennsylvania, New Jersey, New York, or other Northern States, the largest sets that can be obtained (provided they are not large enough to go to flower) we find make the best bulbs. Such sets are usually an inch long, and about half an inch in diameter at the thickest part.

Great care is necessary in harvesting Tuberose bulbs. They should never be placed in heaps large enough to generate heat. In Southern latitudes they can be dried in the open air; but North, the green-house benches or dry air sheds are a necessity. We find the safest way to keep them, after being dried, is to place them closely together, tops up, in single layers, in a dry, warm shed, or in some place under the benches in a green-house, where they will be safe from water.

CALLA, EGYPTIAN LILY, LILY OF THE NILE, (Richardia.)

Calla, the now popular name of this genus, was given to it by Pliny, and by this name it is still known, though the white species, universally cultivated, is now known to botanists as *Richardia Æthiopica*. It is a native of the Cape of Good Hope, and was introduced into England in 1731. It is of easy culture ; the only particular attention it requires is abundance of moisture when in a growing state, and as warm a room as can conveniently be given it ; say an average temperature of 70°.

The Calla is largely grown for winter flowers, and is of the easiest culture. Although it will grow and flower during the entire season without resting if sufficiently fed by being re-potted, yet it is more profitable to dry it partially off, say from June 1st to September 1st. This is best done by placing the pots on their sides, so as to prevent the rains from wetting the soil, and covering them slightly with hay or moss, so as to keep the sun from drying the roots too much ; or, if a position of partial shade can be had, there will be no need of covering the pots. The roots thus rested will flower more abundantly and produce fewer leaves, and thus twice the number of flowers may be obtained from the same space.

It is not well to give the Calla too much pot room, else too much foliage is produced. We have found the best method to be not to use too large pots, and to use liquid manure freely, made from one bushel of cow dung to twenty-five or thirty gallons of water, or one pound of guano to ten gallons of water. When an excess of leaves occurs, cut them off freely, withholding water somewhat for a week or so after cutting the leaves off. By this method the plants can be grown closely together, and a larger crop of flowers obtained from the same space.

The Calla is one of the best of winter-flowering plants for room culture, needing little care beyond abundant water, and an occasional syringing or washing of the leaves, to keep them free from dust and red spider. It is also a good plant for a large aquarium. *R. albo-maculata*, a species with beautifully variegated or spotted foliage, makes a showy plant. The flowers are smaller than the Calla, and white, with purple throat. It comes into flower in June, making it valuable for a succession. It is also desirable in a collection of plants with variegated foliage. Another species, *R. hastata*, is somewhat similar to *R. albomaculata*, except that the flowers are deep yellow with a purple throat. There is still another kind of "Calla," sometimes called the "Black Calla," from the very dark crimson of its velvet-like flowers. It is really, however, a plant of another genus, known as *Arum Palestinum*. It is quite a scarce plant as yet, but will be a great acquisition from its unique and novel color. Unlike most species of the genus *Arum*, the flowers of this are of a pleasing fragrance. (See *Arum*.) The species are all propagated by offsets, which should be taken off when the plant is at rest, and grown on in small pots for one season.

THE AMARYLLIS, (Amaryllis.)

THESE are bulbous plants, mostly natives of the Cape of Good Hope and South America, but which have been increased in number tenfold by hybrids and varieties raised in England and on the Continent. All the kinds are eminently ornamental, and they are all easy of culture, the great secret being to give them alternately a season of excitement and a season of repose. To do this effectually, the plants should be abundantly supplied with water and heat, and placed near the glass when they are coming into flower, and water should be withheld from them by degrees when they are done flowering, till they have entirely ceased growing, when they should be kept quite dry and in a state of rest. When in this state they may be placed in any obscure part of a green-house where it is dry, and of a temperature not under forty or fifty degrees. If kept in such a situation during winter, some kinds may be turned out into a warm border in spring, where they will flower; and if the season be fine, they will renew their bulbs in time to be taken up before the approach of frost.

The chief value of these plants, however, is to produce flowers in the winter season, which they readily do if they are kept dry and dormant during the latter part of the summer and autumn. Indeed, by having a large stock of these bulbs, a regular succession of flowers may be procured during every month in the year. When the dormant bulbs are intended to be thrown into flower, they should be fresh potted in sandy loam and leaf mould, and put in a hot-house or hot-bed, kept rather dry, and covered up with leaves until the pot is well filled with roots, just as is done in forcing Hyacinths or Lilies, except, in the case of Amaryllis, the temperature requires to be kept ten degrees higher, the heat beginning at fifty degrees, and ascending to sixty or seventy degrees; and when the leaves appear, the plants should be abundantly supplied with water. Our long and warm summers enable us to cultivate many of these

AMARYLLIS. (Vittata Type.)

beautiful bulbs in the open air, merely protecting the roots in the winter in the same manner as those of the Dahlia.

THE CROCUS, (Crocus.)

THE Crocus is divided into two classes : the first, those that flower in early spring, too well known to need description ; the second, the autumnal flowering, or naked Crocus, so called because the flowers are produced in the absence of leaves, which, with the seeds, are thrown up in the spring.

The spring Crocus is of the easiest culture, and we need only remark, that it is a mistake to put them into poor ground, since no plants in our gardens delight more in, or make greater returns for, rich soil. They require a dry situation, and in such a place and soil they flower profusely. The bulbs or corms should be planted at least three inches deep ; for, as the new corm forms above the old one, they will in three or four years push themselves out of the ground if planted too near the surface. As often as once in three years the corms should be taken up, separated, and planted out as quickly as possible; the longer they are left out of ground the weaker they become, and the later they will come into bloom.

In starting a new bed, the corms should be planted as soon as they can be obtained, which is usually about the first of September. If left until November, as is the too common practice, very few will flower strongly the coming season, and none satisfactorily. When left in the ground they commence new life about the first of September, and before winter they have their preparations for spring work complete ; the flower buds will be nearly their full length above the bulb, ready for the first sunny days in March to break forth into bloom.

The situation for the Crocus bed should be a warm one, and before hard frosts it may be mulched two or three inches with leaves or coarse litter, which is to be taken off as soon in spring as the season will warrant. The mulching, however, may be omitted where it is not convenient to apply it. *C. sativus*, which is the type of the autumnal flowering species, should be planted in midsummer, and it will come into flower in September. All the species and varieties are increased by offsets. Their introduction into British gardens dates back as far as 1600. The new named varieties introduced recently bear very large flowers, and are, in all respects, very great improvements upon the older kinds.

THE IRIS, (Iris.)

THERE are three distinct kinds of Iris, besides innumerable species, hybrids, and varieties. These are, the fibrous-rooted kinds, which grow best in a fine, sandy loam, and which increase rapidly every year by suckers from the roots; the tuberous-rooted kinds, which are very apt to be destroyed by snails, or to rot from too much wet; and the bulbous kinds, which should be taken up and replanted every second or third year, as the new bulbs, which are formed every season, are always directly under the old bulb; and thus in the course of a few years the bulbs descend so low as to be out of the reach of the air, and consequently incapable of vegetation. Thus it will be generally found that persons in the habit of growing Irises are always complaining of losing their plants, this being the cause. The bulbous and tuberous-rooted Irises succeed in any light and dry soil. The splendid Chalcedonian Iris is one of the tuberous-rooted kinds; and it not only requires a dry soil during winter, but to be allowed plenty of pure air during the whole period of its growth, or it will be very apt to damp off.

Among the species of late introduction is *I. Kœmpfcrii*, from Japan. The plants are perfectly hardy, and are very free-flowering. The flowers are double and single, the colors pure white, purple, maroon, blue, and many with the various colors marbled with white. They grow readily in almost any situation, in full exposure to sun, or in partial shade. They are increased by division, or may be grown readily from seed, which, if sown in the open border, will make plants that will flower the second year. These are really grand plants, and worthy of a place in all gardens. That they do not flower until near midsummer, when the season of the common Iris is past, will be an additional recommendation to most lovers of plants. Another species, *I. Robinsonii*, from New Zealand, is dwarfer than the preceding, and produces beautiful orchid-like flowers. It is yet very rare.

THE CYCLAMEN, (Cyclamen.)

THIS genus contains some of our most popular and desirable plants for fall, winter, and early spring flowering. They are all neat and dwarf in habit; all have foliage of pretty form and beautiful markings, and the flowers in every case are beautiful, some exquisitely so. *C. Persicum* stands at the head of the family, and is the one in most general cultivation.

The Cyclamen should be grown from seed, which

should be sown as soon as ripe in pans or shallow boxes filled with a compost of well-rotted manure, leaf mould, and coarse sand thoroughly incorporated. As soon as the plants have made two leaves, prick out, at one inch apart, into similar pans or boxes filled with the same compost,

CYCLAMEN.

and place upon the shelf in the green-house, near the glass, and shade from direct sunlight. Carefully water; to dry them or drown them is equally fatal. As soon as the plants are well rooted, shift into a three-inch pot, observing the same instructions in all respects. By the first of September they will require a five-inch pot. With proper care and attention, they will be in flower from November through the entire winter months. They require a more even temperature than is usually given to green-house plants, not above 60° nor below 50°; with it bulbs two inches in diameter can be grown in one year.

After flowering they should be gradually ripened off, but never allowed to become thoroughly dry. During summer keep them in a frame, shaded, and give occasionally a little water. They should be repotted again about the first of September, without breaking the ball, and the next flowering will be their perfection of bloom. This species is a native of Persia. All the species are famous for their acridity, yet in Sicily the Cyclamen is the principal food of the wild boars ; hence the common name of *Sow-bread.*

THE RANUNCULUS, (Ranunculus.)

THE species may be divided into two kinds: border flowers and florists' flowers. The latter consist of some hundreds of varieties obtained from the species *Ranunculus Asiaticus*, a native of the Levant, with tuberous roots, which is rather too tender to endure the winter in the Northern States in the open air without some kind of protection. The wild plant grows naturally in Persia, in meadows which are moist during winter and in the growing season, but dry during a great part of summer.

The usual season for planting the Ranunculus is November. The roots may be placed about six inches apart each way, covered with two inches of soil, and protected by straw, mats, or rotten tan, during severe frosts, or they do splendidly when grown in cold frames. The plants will come into flower in June, and when the leaves wither the roots may be taken up, dried in the shade, and preserved in a dry place until they are wanted for replanting. As the plant seeds freely, even when semi-double, new sorts without end may be raised from seed, which may be sown in pots or flat pans as soon as it is gathered, and placed in a cold frame.

The tubers, if kept dry, will retain their vitality for two or three years; and hence, if roots which should be planted in November are kept out of the ground till the November following, and then planted in pots and protected from frost, and when they appear above ground put into green-house heat, they will flower at Christmas. If not planted till December, they will flower about the end of January; and if not planted till January, they will flower in March. In this way, by always having a stock of old roots, and planting some every month in the year, Ranunculuses may be had in flower all the year round. The common mode of propagating the Ranunculus is by separating the offsets from the larger roots.

Several of the species are weeds with us, and common in moist pastures, having been introduced from Europe at an early day. They have become extensively naturalized, so much so as to be a nuisance to farmers in some places. They are popularly known as Buttercups. *R. bulbosus*, a double-flowering species, would be regarded as an acquisition to the flower garden if it were half as difficult to get as it is to be got rid of when once established.

THE WIND FLOWER, (Anemone.)

THE species are showy flowering plants, valued for their hardy nature, and also because they will flower at any required season, according to the time the roots are kept out of the ground. The roots of the Anemone are solid, flattened masses, closely resembling ginger. They should be planted in the garden as early in the spring as possible, in very rich soil, and in partial shade. When the tops are dead, take up and store in a dry, airy place, where they will keep well for two years without injuring their vitality. For in-door cultivation they can be planted at any time in very rich soil in pots or boxes, or cold frames, such as are used for Pansies.

The prevailing colors are red, white, and blue; flowers double or semi-double. One of the earliest spring flowers is *A. nemorosa*, the white Wind Flower of our woods. *A. pulsatilla* and its varieties, with whitish, violet, and purple flowers, are known in cottage gardens as *Pasque Flowers*. *Anemone fulgens*, the scarlet Wind Flower, is the most brilliant and beautiful of all winter and spring flowering Anemones.

THE CROWN IMPERIAL, FRITILLARY,
(Fritillaria.)

SHOWY bulbs for the border, mostly attaining a height of from two to three feet, though *F. meleagris* and its varieties are dwarf. This species, and one or two others like it, have had much attention paid them by florists in Europe, who have succeeded in obtaining many beautiful varieties by seed, and now these flowers occupy a prominent place in their catalogues.

They delight in very rich soil, frequently dug and well pulverized previous to planting. The bulbs may be placed in the ground either in autumn or early spring, covering them with about three inches of earth.

In the blooming season, should the weather prove dry, the ground must be frequently well soaked with water, that the growth may be sufficiently vigorous, or the flowers of the following season will be deficient in size. When the stems begin to decay, the bulbs should be taken up, but not dried to any extent, it being far preferable to preserve them till the following planting season in sand or light and partially dried earth. *F. imperialis* is the well-known Crown Imperial, a native of Persia, of which there are several varieties. They will be greatly benefited by mulching with leaves to the depth of six inches, just before the ground freezes up. They can remain a number of years without being taken up.

THE SNOW-DROP, (Galanthus.)

G. nivalis, the common Snow-drop, for its poetical associations as the ever-welcome harbinger of spring, is universally cultivated, and by potting and very gentle forcing may be made an interesting ornament to the green-house in mid-winter. It is perfectly hardy, however. Loudon remarks: "It is rather singular, and also to be regretted, that no variations or hybrids have been produced from this early and pretty little flower." By way of episode, we may mention that there are but two species of the genus and one variety, but it is probable that a cross might be obtained between it and the allied genus *Leucojum*, or, indeed, other genera of the same order, the great difficulty being, however, to have the different species in flower at the same time. The earliness of the Snow-drop putting it out of the question in a natural manner, it would be necessary to retard the latter till the blooming season of the genus to be selected. Natives of Great Britain.

NASTURTIUM, (Tropæolum.)

An extensive genus of hardy annuals and green-house tuberous and herbaceous perennials, all natives of tropical America. The tuberous-rooted varieties are confined to Peru. The well-known annual plants called the Nasturtium are common in every garden, and only require sowing with the other hardy annuals in spring. There were formerly only two kinds of the annual Tropæolums, *T. major* and *T. minor*, but since 1830 numerous varieties have been raised. One, with very dark flowers, is called *T. minor atrosanguineum*, and another, with dark stripes, is *T. minor venustum*. The young shoots of these plants are succulent, and taste like the common land Cress, the botanical name of which is Nasturtium, and hence they have received their popular name.

Besides the hardy annual kinds, there are several tender tuberous species, most of which are kept in the green-house. The best known of these is *Tropæolum tricolorum*, with flowers marked red, black, and yellow, which has tuberous roots, and such very weak and slender stems, that it is found necessary always to train them over a wire frame, as they are quite unable to support themselves. In Paxton's "Magazine of Botany" it is stated that the tuber of the root should not be buried, but only placed on the surface of the soil, so that the fibrous roots may penetrate it. This, it is said, will enlarge the size of the tuber in "a truly astonishing manner;" and though the plants will not appear healthy the first season, they will afterward become extremely vigorous. It is also recommended to use double pots for these plants, and fill up the interstices with river sand, which should always be kept moist. Substantially the same plan has been followed in this country for many years, and found to succeed well. *T. brachyceras* may be treated in the same manner, and it would probably succeed with *T. tuberosum*, a species which it is very difficult to throw into flower under ordinary treatment, but which grows best in the open ground, in rich soil, and with plenty of air and light.

T. peregrinum, the Canary Bird Flower, was formerly considered a green-house plant, but it is now found much better to treat it as a half-hardy annual, raising the seeds on a hot-bed, and planting them out in May near some trellis-work or other support, which the plant will soon cover in the most graceful manner, producing hundreds of its elegant, fringe-like, pale-yellow flowers. It is propagated from cuttings and by seeds.

ARUM, (Arum.)

THERE are several interesting species contained in this genus, which may be accounted pretty additions to the collections of the hot-house and green-house, though most of the flowers possess a disagreeable odor. In contrast with the other species is *A. Palestinum*, that has flowers of deep crimson, with a delicious fragrance not unlike the Violet. In shape it resembles *Calla Æthiopica;* in fact, when it was introduced, in 1876, into the United States, it was under the name of "Black Calla." They are easily cultivated in sandy loam, and should have a liberal supply of water. Numerous offsets are usually produced, by which the species are extended. *A. dracunculus*, the Dragon Arum, deserves a place in the flower garden for its large and very remarkable flowers. This variety requires the same treatment as the Gladiolus.

The roots of all this natural order, when green, contain a milky fluid, which is exceedingly acrimonious, exciting a painful sensation of burning heat in the tongue and mouth. When cut in slices and applied to the skin, it will very quickly produce a blister. This same active principle is not confined to the roots of the various genera and species, but is found in the leaves as well. A piece of the Calla leaf, not larger than a pin's head, if taken into the mouth, will produce violent and painful burnings. By drying, these roots lose all their poisonous properties, and some of the species yield an excellent quality of Arrow-root.

IXIA, (Ixia.)

A GENUS of beautiful Cape bulbs, with narrow leaves, and slender, simple, or slightly branched stems, bearing spikes of large showy flowers, various in color, and exceedingly attractive when fully expanded by sunshine. *I. viridiflora*, which has large sea-green flowers with black markings at the base of the segments, is a very singular-looking, as well as very beautiful plant. There are many species and some varieties, and the greater part of them are worthy of cultivation. They are half hardy, but with us should be grown in pots in the greenhouse. About midwinter they will begin to show their handsome flowers freely. When done flowering they should be dried off till September or October, which is the proper time to start them again. They grow well in a light loam with the addition of leaf mould and sand. They are propagated by offsets.

GUERNSEY LILY, (Nerine.)

SHOWY bulbous plants, the type of which is the Guernsey Lily, and which are natives of the Cape of Good Hope, China, and Japan. The Guernsey Lily is a native of Japan, and the reason why it has obtained its English name is said to be, that a ship laden with these bulbs and other plants from China was wrecked on the coast of Guernsey; and the bulbs being washed on shore, took root in the sandy soil of the beach, and flourished there so remarkably as to be supposed to be natives of the island. Whether this story be true or not, it is quite certain that for nearly two hundred years these bulbs have been cultivated in Guernsey with the greatest success, growing freely in the open air, and producing an abundance of offsets every year, from which the market is supplied.

The bulbs are usually planted in September and October, in pots of very sandy loam, and placed in the greenhouse or in a window where they will have plenty of light. They will flower in December and January, and remain in flower for a long time. After flowering, and when the leaves begin to turn yellow, water should be gradually withheld till the bulbs are ripe. During the summer, while the bulbs are dormant, the pots may be kept in the green-house or placed in the open air, the latter being the better way. Shift into a larger sized pot about the beginning of September, or earlier if the bulbs show signs of growing, but do not break up the cluster of bulbs, or disturb the roots more than is necessary to break away a portion of the old soil. Water moderately till growth has freely started. The true Guernsey Lily is *N. sarniensis.*

SPARAXIS, (Sparaxis.)

THIS genus is fast rising in the estimation of both the florist and the gardener. Varieties, very pleasing in color, are annually raised in Europe. It is a dwarf bulbous family of plants from the Cape of Good Hope, producing flowers about the size and shape of those of the Crocus, the colors of which are now of infinite variety; pure white, yellow, orange, red, purple, and violet, are to be found, either separate or blended in pleasing variations. They succeed best planted in a frame, where they can have a slight protection during winter. They succeed well also grown in pots in a cool green-house. The bulbs should be potted in September, and kept under a bench until they begin to grow, when they should be given light and water. Three or four bulbs may be put into a five-inch pot with good effect. They increase rapidly by offsets.

BABIANA, (Babiana.)

A GENUS of Cape plants, with solid bulbs or corms, which are eaten by the Hottentots, and which, when roasted, are said to resemble chestnuts. All the species have showy flowers of various colors, blue predominating. Some of the varieties are finely variegated. They succeed in very sandy loam, and may be grown either in pots for ornamenting the green-house, or planted in a cold frame, where, if protected from frost in winter, they may be allowed to remain altogether. They increase rapidly by offsets.

THE AMAZON LILY, (Eucharis.)

THIS is a free-growing bulbous plant of rare beauty and delicious fragrance. It should be grown in the hot-house or a warm green-house. The flowers are produced in a truss of from four to eight, according to the strength of the bulb and the manner of treatment, and are borne on a stem that lifts them just above the leaves. They are pure waxy white, and of great substance. The species are of comparatively recent introduction, and owing to a general impression that they are difficult to manage, are but little grown. The plant is found growing by the side of a river; consequently, moisture and heat are essential to the development of its flowers. The ease with which it is now cultivated, and the fact that a dozen or more large pots of it will furnish flowers nearly the whole year, make it invaluable in all collections of choice plants.

The plants may be potted at any time of the year, taking care not to damage the bulbs or roots, and removing as much of the old soil as possible. The soil should be composed of loam, leaf mould, sand, and well-rotted manure in equal proportions. Give the pots liberal drainage. While they are growing freely they should have plenty of water and liquid manure twice a week. They should be syringed twice a day. The temperature of the house during winter should not fall below 70°, and the plants should have a good share of sunshine.

If wanted to flower during the winter months, water should be used sparingly from August to October. The bulbs should be disturbed as little as possible, repotting when necessary, without division. Side shoots may be taken off at any time and potted in small pots, and, if well managed, they will flower in a year. The green fly and thrips are apt to trouble them. They should be sponged off or got rid of by smoking every alternate day for a week.

The three species at present known are *E. grandiflora*, the largest and best, *E. Amazonica*, and *E. candida*, a small-flowering species, but very beautiful. They all require the same general treatment. The plant was first introduced in 1864.

THE OXALIS, (Oxalis.)

THIS genus comprises a great number of species, differing widely in their habits and manner of growth. Some are annuals, some herbaceous perennials, and some greenhouse shrubs. Many have tuberous roots, and others are bulbs. Some are tender, and others perfectly hardy. The flowers are always handsome in form and beautiful in color. The leaves vary considerably, but they are mostly trifoliate and slightly acid. Many of the species are grown in the green-house, one of the most useful being *O. floribunda*, which was introduced from Brazil in 1829. This very beautiful species requires the protection of the green-house during the winter. It has bright rose-colored flowers, which are produced in great abundance during nearly the whole year. There is a variety of this species with pure white flowers. Both are rapidly increased by division of the root.

Of the bulbous species, *O. Bowiei* is decidedly the handsomest. The flowers are large and of a brilliant rose color, and produced in the greatest profusion. There is also a white variety of this species. *O. Bowiei* is generally cultivated as a green-house plant; it will, however, endure our winters if planted in a rockery or in the border; and so tenacious is it of life that it will dispute possession with almost any other plant in the bed. This species was introduced from the Cape of Good Hope in 1824. Another most desirable kind for conservatory decoration is *O. lutea*, also a Cape species, with large terminal clusters of golden yellow flowers on long, slender scapes. *O. versicolor* is still another beautiful species. It requires the sunlight to expand its flowers; but they are generally thought to be more beautiful when closed than when open. The colors are crimson, white, and a pale shade of yellow. It is rapidly increased by offsets. There is a number of other species that deserve a place in the green-house. They are all of the easiest culture, and grow freely in a sandy loam. The bulbous species take a season of rest, and should be potted in fresh soil in September or October.

SQUILLS, SCILLAS, (Scilla.)

An extensive genus of very pretty bulbous plants, nearly all of which are hardy, and very desirable on account of their early habit of flowering. They should be planted in October, either in the open ground or in pots. They prefer a light, rich soil. *S. campanulata* is a native of Spain, and has beautiful blue flowers, of which there are varieties with white and pink flowers. *S. amœna*, with

THE SQUILL. (Scilla.)

blue flowers, from the Levant, is a very early flowering species. *S. bifolia*, with red, blue, or white flowers. *S. Sibirica*, with intense blue flowers.

These are all beautiful plants, and well adapted to the open border. They come into flower with the Crocus, and continue in bloom much longer. They may remain undisturbed where planted for a number of years, as crowding from their natural increase does not seem to injure them. *S. Peruviana* is one of the best for pot culture. It is a native of Italy and Spain, and not of Peru, as is generally supposed, and as its name would imply. Its flowers are dark blue, and produced in long racemes. *S. ciliaris* is also desirable for growing in pots. The last two are not hardy. All the species are well worth a place in the garden or the green-house.

WINDOW GARDENING, BASKET PLANTS,
AND
CARE OF PLANTS IN ROOMS.

No one, unless engaged in the business extensively, as we are, can have any conception of the extent to which plants are used for window gardening, so-called, and also for the decor.tion of the sitting-room or parlor during the fall, winter, and spring months.

WINDOW BOXES.

Window gardening, as it is done in England—and it is yet there done much better than with us—consists in having boxes fitted so as to rest on the window sill *outside* the window; these, of course, being used only at those seasons when it is warm enough for plants to be placed outside. Such boxes may be made of wood, terra-cotta, iron, or wire patterns. The latter are probably the best, as they give free drainage for water, and for the easy admission of air to the roots. A simple and cheap window box is often made of square slats an inch or so in thickness. These are placed at from half an inch to an inch apart at the bottom and sides. This, like the wire window box, gives ample drainage, which is always a great advantage to the plants; for, besides freely allowing the water to pass off, the spaces allow the air to get through the soil to the roots, a most valuable advantage to the health of the plants. As in wire boxes, moss, or some such material, must be placed against the slat-work, to prevent the soil washing through when watering. No matter what material the window box be made of, outlets for water must be provided, either by making holes an inch or so in diameter, at distances of six inches apart, on the bottom, or making the bottom of slats placed half an inch or so apart.

Window boxes are often made to be quite ornamental, but this is of little consequence, for if the plants in them are properly grown, they will be the most attractive ornament; and as drooping plants are essential to the beauty of the window box, these quickly cover up all parts of it. The length and breadth of the window box, of course, should conform to the size of the sill, but it should never exceed six inches in depth.

Soil.

There is nothing special in the soil used for window boxes; the same rule applies here as for plant culture in pots. The best soil is what is called a turfy, sandy loam; that is, the soil formed by rotted sods that have been cut two inches thick from some good pasture land. That, with the addition of one-fourth rotted stable manure well mixed through it, will answer for almost any plant grown. But it is often troublesome to get the materials to compost small quantities of soil, and it is usually the best plan to get what soil is wanted, either for window boxes or the potting of plants, from the nearest florist.

Kinds of Plants.

When the window box is placed at a great height from the street, it is essential that the colors used should be of the brightest, particularly those that droop or hang over. An excellent combination is made by planting the first or inner row of *Scarlet Geraniums*, the middle row of the *Golden Feather* plant, while the outer or drooping line should be of *Lobelia gracilis*, which has flowers of rich blue, drooping, when well grown, from one and a half to two feet. Another style is to plant the inside line with *pink Geraniums*, the middle line of the "Rainbow Plant," as it is sometimes called, (*Alternanthera parychoides major,*) the leaves of which are tinted yellow, violet, crimson, orange, etc., and the drooping or. outer line of *scarlet Tropæolums*. Sometimes a mixed variety is preferred, which may be made of *Heliotropes, Lemon Verbenas, Fuchsias,* or such plants as taste dictates, having the finer kinds of *Verbenas, Petunias,* or *scarlet Nasturtiums* to droop. The plants should be set out about five or six inches' apart.

Window boxes are often used to grow annual plants only, from seed, such as *Mignonette, Sweet Alyssum, Asters, Portulaca, Drummond's Phlox,* etc. These may either be sown separately, or two or three kinds may be sown in rows in the same box. If several kinds are sown, the drooping, such as *Phlox*, should be the outside line. After having the box filled with proper soil, draw a furrow in it about half an inch deep, and in that sow the seed, the ordinary sized packet being enough. Cover the soil carefully over it, and then press the soil so as to moderately firm the seed. *When dry*, water gently with a fine rose watering pot. If the seeds are sown in the window boxes inside the house, it may be done any time in April; but if not so soon wanted, the boxes are placed outside, and the sowing deferred till May.

After the seedlings or plants have grown so as to be well established in the boxes, they should be copiously watered once every other day. If the weather be dry, and the boxes are exposed to the full glare of the noonday sun, no light sprinkling will answer; the water must be poured on until it runs out at the bottom of the box. If, however, they are partly shaded, or if the weather be cloudy or wet, judgment, of course, must be used in the matter of watering. The rule with all plants in pots or boxes is, never to water until the soil is dry, and then water thoroughly. This dryness can be determined by the soil getting lighter in color, or by examination by stirring it up with the fingers.

HANGING BASKETS.

These may be formed of materials similar to those used for window boxes, although the usual kinds are such as are formed of rustic work and wire. These last are rather the best suited for the health of the plants; for, as in window boxes so made, they allow full opportunity for the free passage of water from the soil, and for the admission of air to the roots. As hanging baskets are exposed on all sides to the air, they will require more attention in watering than window boxes. The simplest and most efficient way, after the plants have become well established, is, when dry, to immerse the whole basket in a tub of water. This is particularly essential, if the basket is made of wire or any such material. Rustic baskets, of course, do not drain off so freely, and immersing them in water is not so essential, so that the rule for watering window boxes may be adapted to them. The plants for hanging baskets may be similar to those used for window boxes, except that it conduces much to the appearance of the baskets to have some graceful plant placed in the center of each for that purpose. Nothing is better than some of the Palms or Dracænas. Of Palms,

Latania borbonica and *Corypha australis* are excellent; and of *Dracænas, D. terminalis,* with its crimson leaves, and *D. indivisa,* with its drooping green, fountain-like foliage, are good types, though there are scores of others, prominent among which are the fancy leaved *Caladiums, Rex Begonias,* and *Crotons,* for partially shaded verandas. If the basket has handles, some climbing plant, such as *Ivy* or *Climbing Fern,* etc., may be trained on these, while the plants used for drooping over the sides may be such as are advised for window boxes.

If baskets or vases are in very exposed situations, such as cemeteries, where water cannot be easily given, it is best to use succulent plants, such as *Echeverias* and *Sempervivums,* (House Leek,) for the centers of the vases or baskets, and for the pendent plants, some of the beautiful forms of the *Mesembryanthemums* or *Sedums,* (Stone-crop.) All of these plants thrive with comparatively little moisture when once established in the soil, and present a good appearance, even if watered copiously only once a week in the driest weather.

PLANTS IN ROOMS.

Although plants can now be purchased almost everywhere at very low rates, it is always a satisfaction to the housewife who is a lover of plants to know that the plant she now admires and cares for was of her own creation ; that she herself raised it from a slip or a seed. But as the best modes of propagating plants would involve too much space in this article, I must refer such as need instruction on the raising of plants from slips or seeds to the article on *The Propagation of Plants,* page 67. But whether the plants have been raised at home or purchased from the florist, it is all important that they be in vigorous health to start with, or success is not likely to ensue; for once a plant gets unhealthy, it is a loss of labor to attempt to get it again in health. It is better to throw it away, and start again with healthy slips, seeds, or plants.

If the young plants have not been raised at home, by slips or seeds, it is always better to purchase young, healthy plants than large plants that have been forced into flower, although we well know that, with the great majority of plant cultivators, this advice will be thrown away, as five people out of six buy only plants in flower. It is really far better for the purchaser to be guided by catalogue descriptions than to buy plants that hav been forced into flower at a high temperature.

Supposing, then, that the plant has been purchased from the florist, and has been growing in a pot three inches deep and wide, it is usually in a condition to require a larger pot, which will be known by observing that the roots mat the outside of the ball of earth. Such a plant, whether it be a Rose, Geranium, Fuchsia, or any other similar free-growing plant, will require a pot one or two inches wider than that it has been grown in. It is usually the safest plan to shift it into only one size larger; but if two sizes larger are used, then at least an inch of "drainage" should be placed in the bottom of the pot, so that the water can pass freely from the greater mass of soil. This drainage may consist of charcoal, broken pots, oyster shells, etc. If the plant has been only placed in a pot one inch larger than it has been growing in, then there is no need for drainage. We ourselves never use drainage in our flower pots, unless for some reason we are obliged to give them an extra large pot, when the drainage is used to counteract the evil effects of using a too large pot.

Repotting.

The indication that a plant needs repotting into a size larger pot is known by knocking it out of the pot, by giving a smart rap on the edge of a board, just as is done in taking a form of jelly out of a mould. If the roots have become matted on the outer surface of the ball of earth, then it is in a condition to require a larger sized pot. For the soil to use in potting, that recommended for window boxes will answer equally well for plants in pots. We are often asked if saucers should be used to stand pots in. As a matter of keeping the place clean where the plants stand, it is a necessity ; but the saucers should never be filled with water, unless when sub-aquatic plants are grown, such as *Agapanthus, Callas, Hyacinths, Tradescantias*, or other plants of similar character. The best temperature for parlor plants is about 55° at night, which may be increased to 10 or 15 degrees higher during the day.

Aspect.

The best aspect for plants grown in rooms is east or southeast, south or southwest, but never north. It is necessary, once in eight or ten days, to turn the plants, so that each side gets an equal share of light, else the plants will get lop-sided. If plants drop their leaves, or the leaves become yellow, it is usually owing to one of two causes : either that the soil is too wet or too dry. Either condition will destroy the small rootlets, which is indicated by the condition of the leaves. There is usually more injury done from the plants being too wet than too dry.

INSECTS.

There are only three insects that are really troublesome to parlor plants, the *aphis*, or *green fly*, the *red spider*, and the *mealy bug*. The first is easily destroyed by tobacco in any form, either as liquid, dust, or by smoke. The most convenient way to use it for house plants, is to first wet the leaves, then dust snuff or tobacco dust over them. The *red spider* insect is not quite so easy to manage. It never appears unless the air is hot and dry, when it attacks the lower side of the leaves. The best remedy is to wash the leaves off with a sponge; or, if the plants are very large, lay the plants on their side, and strike the leaves forcibly with water from a syringe or hose. The *mealy bug* insect looks like little bits of white cotton, and is usually found at the axils of the leaves. It is best removed by a strong hair pencil, after which syringe or sponge the plant.

All these instructions refer to plants that are grown in rooms from October until May. After that date, if circumstances permit, the plants should be shifted into good sized pots, and placed in the open garden, sinking the pots in the earth to the rim, care being taken to pinch out the leading shoots of the plants, so as to make them grow into good shape. If the pots are sunk in the ground in this way, care must be taken to have them turned around every two or three weeks, else the roots will get through the hole in the bottom of the pot, which would have to be broken off, and this would seriously injure them. Perhaps the best way is to stop up the hole entirely, so that the roots cannot get through. A cork is best for this purpose, as it must be taken out if the plants are again used as house plants.

Many plants, such as *Geraniums, Heliotropes, Abutilons,* all the *Coleuses, Ageratums,* and similar strong growing plants, usually get too large for house plants the second year, and it is better with all such to use young slips, or procure young plants of them in the fall; while such plants as *Carnations, Roses, Azaleas, Camellias, Jessamines,* etc., are better when older, if they have been properly cared for. One of the most popular house plants for fall and the early winter months is the *Chrysanthemum,* of which there is now an endless variety, embraced in the three types known as "Large Flowering," "Japan," and "Bouquet" or "Pompone." They are grown with the greatest ease; and if the flower buds are pinched back as late as September 1st, they may be had in bloom nearly to Christmas.

There are a great variety of plant stands and other contrivances on which to set plants in rooms, but as these can best be understood by illustrations, florists' catalogues must be consulted.

Climbing Plants.

Among this class of plants there are some that are well adapted for culture in the sitting-room or the parlor; and these, aside from the small additional trouble of giving them something to climb on, are as easily grown as any other kind of plant, and do well with the same kind of soil and treatment. While some are admired for the beauty of their flowers, the greater number are also valued as furnishing a graceful drapery for the window and its surroundings, and a not less picturesque frame of living green for the plants on the table.

Among the more desirable climbers for room culture is the comparatively new so-called German Ivy, (*Senecio macroglossis*,) a much better plant than the old kind. It is a strong and rapid grower, with glossy leaves that so much resemble those of the common Ivy as to be easily mistaken for it. As free-growing plants of this kind are troublesome to repot when trained, it is a good plan to give them at the beginning a pot sufficiently large to last during the winter, taking the precaution, in this case, to give a sufficient quantity of drainage to prevent the soil from becoming sour. These remarks will apply to all plants of this kind.

Another pretty climber for the room is the popular Smilax, (*Myrsiphyllum asparagoides*,) universally admired for its graceful foliage and the sweetness of its tiny little flowers. It should be repotted in August, or at least as soon as the new growth appears. Shake off all the old soil that will come away, (only do not expose the roots too much,) and replace it with fresh, rich soil.

Still another good climber for room culture is the Japanese Climbing Fern, (*Lygodium scandens*.) The peculiar beauty of this plant is not seen till it gets age, and produces abundantly its lovely fertile fronds. A cool room will suit it better than a hot one.

For training on small wire frames, either flat or round, few plants are more desirable than the Ivy-leaved Geraniums. There are varieties with single, and others with double flowers, of various shades of color. The leaves are of a glossy green, and closely resemble those of the English Ivy. Except that they should be trained to a stake or a frame, they are treated as other Geraniums.

The foliage of all these climbers should be washed off or syringed occasionally, not only to free them from dust, but also from insects, especially the red spider. There are other climbers that do well in rooms, but the above are among the best and easiest grown.

PROPAGATION OF PLANTS

BY

CUTTINGS, LAYERS, DIVISION, AND SEED.

PROBABLY there is no horticultural operation so interesting as that of Propagation. Although I have been at the business now for nearly forty-five years, still there is no part of the work that to me compels such unflagging interest as that of calling into separate existence a dozen, a hundred, or a thousand slips from one plant, or of watching the varied forms of tiny seedling plants when called into separate individual life by the methods used for that purpose. No matter how well able the lover of plants may be to buy them in their full development, they never have the charm that the bantlings of his own raising give. This is particularly the case with amateur florists, who have but a few plants, and who have time enough and interest enough to pet and care for each particular plant.

The following instructions in the art of propagation, I trust, will be so plain and simple that the most inexperienced amateur, as well as the young florist, will be able to understand and follow them. The instructions will contain all our most recent experience; and though some of them will be nearly identical with what I have before written on this subject in the *Hand-book of Plants*, yet there is such additional information (particularly on Rose Propagation) as will be interesting and instructive, I trust, even to such as have already read what I have before written.

Propagation by Cuttings.

This is the way in which the largest number of plants are propagated. As now understood, this is a simple matter. Formerly no operation in horticulture was more befogged by ignorant pretenders, who, in writing or speaking on the subject, so warped the operation with troublesome conditions as to discourage, not only amateurs in horticulture, but inexperienced professional gardeners as well.

One of the first necessary conditions in the propagation of plants by cuttings is, that the plant from which the cutting or slip is taken must be in vigorous health. If weak or tainted by disease, failure is almost certain to result. If, for example, we wish to root cuttings of greenhouse or bedding plants, such as *Bouvardias, Chrysanthemums, Fuchsias, Geraniums, Heliotropes, Salvias, Verbenas,* etc., one of the best guides to the *proper condition* is when the cutting breaks or snaps clean off instead of bending or "kneeing." If it snaps off so as to break, then it is in the condition to root freely; if it bends, it is too old, and though it will root, it will root much slower, and make a weaker plant than the slip that snaps off on being bent. With very few exceptions, and those of but little importance, cuttings of all kinds root freely from slips taken from the *young wood,* that is, the young growth, before it gets hardened, and when in the condition indicated by the "snapping test," as it is called.

I believe I was the first to call attention to this valuable test of the condition of the cutting (snapping) in my work, *Practical Floriculture,* first published in 1868. A very general idea is current that cuttings must be cut at or below an eye or joint. The practice of this system is not only rarely necessary, but it leads undoubtedly to many cases of failure; not that the cutting at or below a joint either hinders or assists the formation of roots, but from the fact that, when a slip is cut at a joint, the shoot often has become too hard at that point, while half an inch higher up, or *above* the joint, the proper condition will be found. I know that it will root even when in the too hard condition, but the roots emitted will be hard and slender, and, as a consequence, will not be likely to make a plant of the same vigor as that made from the cutting in the proper state; besides, as the hard cutting takes a longer time to root, its chances of failing from unfavorable atmospheric conditions are thus increased.

With these instructions for the proper state of the cutting, I now proceed to describe the medium wherein it is to be placed, and the conditions of temperature, moisture, etc. If these are strictly followed, failure is an impossibility; for the laws governing the rooting of a slip are as certain as those governing the germination of a seed. In our own practice, when these conditions are strictly followed, failure is unknown, when the cutting or slip is in the proper condition of health.

The best degree of temperature to root cuttings of the great majority of green-house and bedding plants is 65° of bottom heat, indicated by a thermometer plunged in the sand of the bench, and an atmospheric temperature of 15° less. A range of 10° may be allowed, that is, 5° lower or 5° higher; but the nearer the heat of the sand can be kept to 65°, and that of the rest of the house to 50°, the more perfect the success will be. If a much higher temperature be maintained, it will be at the expense of the ultimate health of the plants. These temperatures refer to propagation under glass from November to April Of course, when the outside temperature is higher these temperatures cannot be maintained.

Sand is the best medium in which to place cuttings; color or texture is of no special importance. What we use is the ordinary sand used by builders; this is laid on the hot-bed or bench of the green-house to the depth of about three inches and firmly packed down. When "bottom heat" is wanted, the flue or pipes under the bench of the green-house are boarded in, so that the heat strikes the bottom of the bench, thus raising the temperature in the sand. We prefer the bottom of the bench to be of slate, as it is a better conductor than boards; but in the absence of slate boards will answer.

From the time the cuttings are inserted in the sand until they are rooted, they should never be allowed to get dry; in fact, our practice is to keep the sand soaked with water until the cutting is just on the point of emitting roots, the cutting bench being watered copiously every morning, and often, when the atmosphere is dry, again in the evening, (when the green-house is artificially heated.) Kept thus saturated, there is less chance of the cutting getting wilted, either by heat from the sun or from fire heat; for if a cutting once gets wilted, its juices are expended, and it becomes in the condition of a hard cutting, the condition in which, when bent, it will not snap nor break, which has already been described. To avoid this wilting or flagging of the cutting, every means that will suggest itself to the propagator is to be used. Our practice is to shade and ventilate in the propagating house or hot-bed just as soon in the forenoon as the action of the sun's rays on the glass raises the temperature of the house to $65°$ or $70°$. Of course, in hot weather the temperature cannot be thus lowered, and for this reason the propagation of plants is a difficult matter during the months of June, July, and August, except such plants as Coleus and others of tropical origin.

This practice of ventilating the propagating house or hot-bed is, I am aware, not in very common use, many contending that the place where the propagating is done should at all times be kept close. I have tried both methods long enough and extensively enough to satisfy myself beyond all question, that ventilating and propagating at a low temperature are capable of producing a larger number of plants during the season than a high temperature and a close atmosphere. There need be no failures; and it has the important advantage of producing a *healthy* stock, which the close or high temperature system would fail to do in the case of many plants. I have often heard propagators boasting of rooting cuttings in five days. I am well aware that this may be done, but I am also aware that it is often done in damp and cloudy weather at the risk of the whole crop, and it must be done at a high temperature, which at all times causes the plants to draw up slender, and thus impairs their vitality.

Fungus of the Cutting Bench.

Permitting a moderate circulation of air in the propagating house tends to prevent the germination of that spider-web-like substance, which, for want of a better term, is known among gardeners as the "*fungus of the cutting bench.*" Every one who has had any experience in propagating knows the baneful effects of this; how that, in one night, it will often sweep off thousands of cuttings that a few hours before were in healthful vigor. But this dangerous enemy of the propagator requires, like vegetation of higher grades, conditions suitable to its development, which are a calm atmosphere and a temperature above 55° or 60°. Hence, to avoid this pest, we make every effort, by shading, airing, and regulation of fire heat, to keep the atmosphere of the house so that it shall not exceed 60 degrees. This, of course, is not practicable when the outside temperature in the shade is above 60°; but the temperature can be reduced considerably by dashing water on the pathways and other parts of the house. It is rarely, however, that the outside temperature ever exceeds 60° at night for any length of time in the vicinity of New York before the middle of May, and all propagating had better be finished previous to that time, unless of tropical plants. In the fall months, about the middle of September, operations in propagating may again begin.

The temperature is prevented from rising in the house in various ways, some using canvas, or bast matting, or syringing the glass with a mixture of naphtha and white lead, made about the color and consistency of thin skim milk. We find, however, the best and most convenient shading to be that formed by flexible screens made of common lath, planed and attached together like Venetian blinds, the laths being an inch or so apart. These can be quickly rolled or unrolled, and give an ever-varying modified shade, sufficiently cooling to the house, yet not darkening the cutting enough to impair its vigor. These are not unrolled in the morning until the temperature inside indicates it to be necessary, and are rolled up in the afternoon as soon as the sun ceases to shine on the glass, for it is of the utmost importance that the cuttings receive as much light as they will bear without becoming wilted. An objection to these screens, however, is their expense, as they cost about ten cents per square foot.

The time required by cuttings to root varies from eight to twenty days, according to the variety, condition of the cutting, and temperature. Verbenas, Fuchsias, or Heliotropes, put in in proper condition, and kept without ever being allowed to wilt, will root, in an average bottom heat of 65°, in eight days, while Roses, Pelargoniums, or Petunias will take at least double that time under the same conditions.

It is best to pot off the cuttings at once when rooted, no matter how small the roots may be; half an inch is a much better length for them to be when potted than two inches, and the operation is much quicker performed when the roots are short than when long. But the main evils of delaying the potting off of cuttings are, that when left too long the cuttings grow up weak and spindling, the roots become hard, and do not take as quickly to the pot. The same care is required in shading and watering after potting, nearly, as in the cutting bench; for no matter how carefully taken up, in the operation of potting the delicate roots get less or more injured, and until the cuttings begin to emit new roots they are nearly as liable to wilt as the unrooted cuttings.

Cuttings should always be placed in small pots, the best size being from two to two and a half inches wide and deep; if placed in larger pots the soil dries out too slowly, and the tender root, imbedded too long in a mass of wet soil, rots, and the plant dies. Though we generally prefer soil to be unsifted in potting large plants, yet for newly-potted cuttings it is better to be sifted fine, not only that it is more congenial thus to the young roots, but also that the operation is quicker done with finely-sifted soil.

After potting, the cuttings are placed on benches covered with an inch or so of sand, watered freely with a fine rose watering pot, and shaded for four or five days; by that time they will have begun to root, when no further shading is necessary.

"Saucer System" of Propagation.

The above methods of propagating by cuttings are such as are now practised by commercial florists, but for amateurs in horticulture, or gardeners who have charge of private green-houses, there is usually no necessity for a regular propagating house, unless the requirements for plants are unusually large, as the *"Saucer System"* of propagation will answer every purpose, and it is the safest of all methods in inexperienced hands. I was, I believe, the first to introduce this system some twenty years ago, and here repeat the directions first given in one of the horticultural journals at that time: Common saucers or plates are used to hold the sand in which the cuttings are placed. This sand is put in to the depth of an inch or so, and the cuttings inserted in it close enough to touch each other. The sand is then watered until it becomes of the condition of mud, and placed on the shelf of the green-house, or on the window-sill of the sitting-room or parlor, fully exposed to the sun, and never shaded. But one condition is essential to success: until the cuttings become rooted *the sand must be kept continually saturated, and kept in the condition of mud;* if once allowed to dry up, exposed to the sun as they are, the cuttings will quickly wilt, and the whole operation will be defeated.

The rules previously laid down for the proper condition of the cuttings are the same in this case, and those for the temperature nearly so; although, by the saucer system, a higher temperature can be maintained without injury, as the cuttings are in reality placed in water, and will not droop at the same temperature as if the sand were kept in the regular condition of moisture maintained in the propagating bench. Still, the detached slip, until rooted, will not endure a continuation of excessive heat, so that we advise, as we do in the regular method of propagating, that the attempt should not be made to root cuttings in this way, in this latitude, in the months of June, July, or August, unless with plants of a tropical nature. When the cuttings are rooted, they should be potted in small pots, and treated carefully by shading and watering for a few days, as previously directed. All kinds of plants may be rooted by this method when the young green wood is used, whether of soft wooded plants, such as Fuchsias, Carnations, Geraniums, Heliotropes, etc., or of hard-wooded plants, such as Roses or Azaleas, provided that the same condition of cutting is adhered to as advised for the other methods.

PROPAGATION OF ROSES BY CUTTINGS.

As the propagation of Roses by cuttings is a matter of very wide-spread interest, I will give a special description of our method. The rule that applies to the proper condition of soft-wooded plants, such as *Fuchsias, Heliotropes*, or *Verbenas*, (that is, that the young shoot should be in a state to snap or break off instead of bend,) does not apply to the proper condition of the Rose cutting. The young shoot of the Rose is also what is to be used, but it must be hard and woody. For example, when a Rose bud is developed enough to be cut, the shoot on which it grows is about in the right condition for cuttings, each leaf of the shoot with its bud at the axil, and two or three inches of stem, making a cutting; that is, what is called a single eye cutting. They are simply made by making one rather slanting cut between the joints, or about a quarter of an inch above the eye. About one-third of the leaf is cut off, mainly for the reason of allowing more cuttings to be put in the cutting bench. If by any accident the leaf is all taken off, a Rose cutting in this condition will never root to make a good plant; or if, from any cause, the leaves drop off while the cuttings are in the process of rooting, not one in ten will ever make a satisfactory plant. Besides the system of using cuttings made from one eye or bud, the "blind wood," so-called, (that is, the shoots that do not produce flower buds,) is also used, and generally makes the safest and best kind of cuttings, as these blind shoots are hard and slender, and root rather quicker than cuttings made from single eyes. These shoots are usually too short-jointed to be made into single eye cuttings, and have often two or more eyes in the cutting; but the foliage should be shortened off about one-third, as in the single eye cuttings. A good length for a Rose cutting is three inches, though in some short-jointed kinds no more than one inch length of cutting can be obtained.

There is no difficulty in propagating Roses from cuttings of healthy young wood, if *it is grown under glass*, any time from September to May; but during the months of June, July, and August, it is a process requiring great care and attention. We, however, grow hundreds of thousands in this way by the following method: About the middle of May we plant out our stock plants on the green-house benches, in four or five inches of rather poor soil, containing not a particle of manure, the object being to induce a hard and slender woody growth of cuttings, instead of a soft and pithy one. Obtaining cuttings of this kind, there is no great difficulty in rooting them. I will state, however, that after they are potted off, carefully shading from the hot sun is necessary until the root strikes through to the side of the pot. I have found it to be a great help in propagating in summer to sift a thin layer of fine moss or cocoanut fiber over the Rose cuttings after potting. This keeps them moist, acting as a mulch, and also, after they have rooted, it keeps them cool in hot weather, both materials being excellent non-conductors.

It is a curious fact that, no matter how healthy Rose cuttings may be when growing in the open ground, they can rarely be got in condition, during the summer months, to root. I have tried them at all seasons and in all conditions, but do not think I ever made a success during the months of June, July, or August. They invariably drop their leaves, and this means failure every time. Why they should do so more than those grown inside, I have never yet been able to discover, but that such are the facts any one trying it will very quickly find out. My experience in this matter has been confined to the latitude of New York. I believe that in some sections of the country, by the shoots becoming better ripened, they may be successfully propagated from out-door wood in the summer.

Hybrid Perpetual and even Monthly Roses, however, can be propagated from cuttings of well-ripened hard wood grown in the open ground, put in in October or November in any place, (a cold green-house or a cold frame,) where they can be kept just above the freezing point at night; say from $32°$ to $40°$, with $10°$ to $15°$ more during the day. They must not get much frost, though a few degrees would do no harm, except to retard them; but artificial heat, for any length of time, above $40°$ to hard wood cuttings is almost certain to destroy them. I remember, some years ago, my foreman insisted that we should put in a lot of the prunings of a lot of new Hybrid Perpetual Roses that we had received in December from Europe, in our regular Propagating House. I told him it was useless; but he insisted on being allowed to try. I gave him the privilege, provided he did the work in his own time at night. He worked most diligently, and got three or four of the hands to help him for a week at nights. He got some 20,000 cuttings in the propagating bench, where the temperature of the sand marked 65°. The cuttings threw out shoots an inch in length, callused beautifully, and up to that point any one that had not gone through the thing before would have said that the operation was a success. One morning, about ten days after being put in, he called me to witness his victory; but I astounded him by saying, that for every plant he made from the 20,000 cuttings I would give him 25 cents. He watched and redoubled his care; but it was no use. In less than a month every cutting had blackened and rotted.

Had the temperature of the sand never exceeded 40°, a large proportion would have rooted; but it would have taken four or five months to do so; and then the results are never so satisfactory as when cuttings are made from the green wood taken from growing plants under glass. When, however, there is no green-house at hand, but only cold frames, such as are used for cabbage or lettuce plants, the hard wood cuttings of Roses placed in such in October will, if not too much frozen, root strongly by April. One of our market gardeners here has followed the plan for twenty years. His cold frames, where he keeps his cabbage plants, are well sheltered, and he roots thousands of Hybrid Perpetual Rose cuttings simply by sticking them between the rows of cabbage plants. He thus gets four or five hundred in a 3×6 sash, without detriment to the cabbage plants, as they are leafless, and look like dried sticks until the cabbage plants are taken out in spring, when they begin to leaf out, and are rooted sufficiently to pot by the 1st of May.

PROPAGATING ROSES IN THE SOUTHERN STATES.

The method of propagating Roses at the South is very simple, particularly in the vicinity of Charleston, S. C., Savannah, Ga., or in almost any part of Florida. There the long, heated summers raise the temperature of the sandy soil as high as the atmosphere in the winter months, if not higher, forming, in fact, a sort of natural hot-bed. All, then, that it is necessary to do in such a case is to make cuttings of Roses, either Monthly or Hybrid Perpetual, into lengths of five or six inches, and make a trench deep enough to plant them, leaving only one or two eyes or buds above ground. Care must be taken to firm the cuttings well in with the foot, so as to exclude the air. The cuttings may be set in the trenches four to six inches apart, and two or three feet between the lines. Cuttings of Roses planted in this way, in these or similar states, in November and December, will form roots by February; and if left to grow where placed without being disturbed, will have made growths of from one to five feet in the following September, according to the variety or class.

PROPAGATION BY LAYERING.

Propagating by layering in the usual way in the soil is but little practised now-a-days, since the ways of rooting plants by cuttings have been so greatly simplified; but occasionally some one may want a few plants of a Rose or other shrub growing in the open ground who has not other ways of propagation at command, when this plan may be safely adopted.

Although layering may be done with the ripened wood of vines or shrubs of the growth of the previous season, yet it is preferable to use the shoot of the present year in its half green state; for example, a Rose or flowering shrub is pruned in the usual way in spring; by June or July it will have made strong shoots one, two, or three feet in length from or near the base of the plant. Take the shoot then in the left hand, (after having stripped it of its leaves for a few inches on each side of where it is to be cut,) keep the fingers under the shoot, and make a clean cut on the *upper part*, an inch or so in length, and to about half the thickness of the shoot, then slightly twist the "tongue" or cut part to one side. Having opened a shallow trench, fasten the branch down with a hooked peg, and cover with earth. It is a good plan to place a flat stone over the layer to prevent the soil from drying out.

This plan of cutting the shoot on the *upper* side I have never seen in illustrations showing the manner of layering, it being usually either on the side or under; but I have found in practice that it is much the safest plan, as the "tongue," when cut on the top part of the shoot, has far less chance to be broken off.

PROPAGATION BY LAYERING IN POTS.

This is the process of layering shoots or runners of plants in pots, so that, when the root forms in the pot, the plant can be detached without injury to it, as the roots are confined exclusively to the soil in the pot. Layering plants in pots can be done with Roses, vines, or shrubs of any kind, with always more certainty of making a plant quicker than by the ordinary way of layering the shoot in the soil, because when lifted there is no disturbance of the roots. This system of propagating Strawberries has been largely practised during the past ten years in the United States, and is now a favorite method. For details, see *Strawberry Culture.*

Propagation by Layering in the Air.

About twenty years ago I published a method of propagating Geraniums. that I believed originated with me, and which I called, for want of a better term, "Layering in the Air." It consists in tonguing the shoot to be used as a cutting half through with a knife, as in the ordinary layering. The shoot so treated forms granulations, or "callus," on the cut surface, and is in a condition to form roots immediately on being detached and put into the earth.

A year or two ago I bethought myself of my long-forgotten plan of "layering in the air," but this time I improved upon the former way of doing it. Instead of tonguing the shoot to be used for a cutting, as before, it was merely snapped short off at a point where the condition of the shoot or slip would make it hang on to the plant by the merest shred of bark. Slight as this strip of bark is, it is sufficient to sustain the cutting, without any material injury from wilting, until it forms the "callus," or granulated condition, which precedes the formation of roots.

The cutting, or slip, may be detached in from ten to twelve days after it has been broken in the manner described, and then potted in two or three inch pots. If watered and shaded rather less than required by ordinary cuttings, it will form roots in ten or twelve days more, and not more than two per cent. will fail. Plants of the Tricolor Geraniums, which all know are difficult to root under the ordinary modes of propagation, particularly in hot weather, do excellently by this plan.

The advantage of this method is not only that the slips root with far greater facility, but the injury to the stock or mother plants is far less than if the slips had been cut clean off instead of being only partly detached. Many other plants can be thus propagated with safety, notably *Begonias*, *Petunias*, *Poinsettias*, and such plants, the cuttings of which have a tendency to damp in hot weather.

PROPAGATION BY DIVISION.

This is the simplest of all methods of increasing plants, but it is almost exclusively confined to hardy herbaceous border plants, although *Cannas*, *Dahlias*, and various other tender plants can also be propagated in this way. But whenever plants are propagated by division, it is best done at their natural period of starting to grow. Thus Phloxes, Chrysanthemums, Pæonias, Iris, and grasses of all kinds start to grow in the Northern States in the open ground about May 1st, which is the best time to divide; while Cannas, Dahlias, and other tender tropical plants should not be divided, if to be set out in the open ground, until a month later, or say the first week in June. In all cases, here as in cuttings, firm the divided roots well with the foot to exclude the air; otherwise the operation may fail.

PROPAGATION BY SEEDS.

The most natural way of increasing plants is by seeds; and whenever it is practicable to do so, it is preferable to all others, so that in our own practice, any plant of which we can procure the seed, we rarely increase in any other way, unless, of course, in cases where particular varieties are wanted that we know will not reproduce themselves from seed, so as to be certain of color or form, for it is believed to be highly probable that no plant ever produces identically the same individual from seed. The resemblance may be so close that, to casual observation, it may seem identical; but reasoning from analogy, it is fair to presume that no generated organism of animal or vegetable life, whether from the lowest molecule to the highest type of existence, is ever identical. No two human beings are ever identical in face or form; and even acquired habits, such as handwriting, are never the same.

Some species of animal and vegetable life, when under domestication, become what is technically termed "broken." Thus we find the pigeon, when domesticated, running into a great variety of plumage, while its prototypes of the woods seem to be all alike; but it is fair to presume they each possess a distinct individuality, though less apparent than the others. So it is in plant life When we sow 1,000 seeds of Verbenas or Coleus, (species that have been "broken,") to the experienced eye no two ever are exactly the same, though the original types from which they sprung will seem to produce varieties identical; but in this case also it is reasonable to presume that a distinct individuality is present, though the distinction is so slight that ordinary observation fails to mark it. The eye requires to be educated to nice distinctions of individuality. Shepherds in charge of five hundred sheep can often individualize every member of the flock, which to the inexperienced observer seem all alike. The reader will excuse this digression; but there is a great deal of misconception on this interesting subject.

In all cases where seed taken from a variety or species

will reproduce itself nearly the same, as in special colors of *Hollyhocks*, or in cases where a general variety is wanted, such as *Verbenas* or *Petunias*, the propagation by seed is largely practised. As propagation by seeds refers more usually to ornamental plants cultivated under glass, I will briefly relate our own practice, which we have greatly improved during the past few years, and in which we have attained almost unfailingly satisfactory results. We have found that seeds sown in shallow boxes, from one and a half to two inches deep, can be given a far more uniform degree of moisture than when sown in earthen flower pots, or earthen seed pans made specially for that purpose. These boxes are made from the ordinary soap box, from four to five being made from each, with the bottom boards so put on as to allow free escape of moisture, though, of course, not so wide apart as to allow the soil to wash through. These boxes are filled with finely sifted soil, such as has been run through a sieve fine as mosquito netting. This surface is then made perfectly level and smooth, and the seeds sowed on it as evenly as possible, and in thickness corresponding to the variety sown, though it must be here remembered that in "union there is strength," and that, if sown too thin, weak seeds may fail to press up the soil if isolated too much. After the seeds are sown, and before they are covered, they are pressed down by a smooth board into the soil, so that the surface is again smooth and level.

The seed box is now ready for its covering. For several years past we have used finely-sifted Moss (Sphagnum) or Cocoanut fiber exclusively for covering. To prepare these materials they are rubbed through a mosquito wire sieve when dry, and sifted over the seed only thick enough to cover it, usually about one-sixteenth part of an inch. In the absence of Moss or Cocoanut fiber, dry refuse hops or leaves will answer, prepared in the same manner, the great object being to use a material light in weight, having non-conducting properties, and that will thus hold the moisture uniformly. Of all these, we now think Cocoanut fiber the best, and use nothing else, as its sponge-like character keeps just the right degree of moisture wanted.

These seed boxes should be placed in the open sunlight, in the windows of the dwelling room, in the hot-bed or green-house, and never shaded, in a temperature running from 55° to 65° at night, with 10° higher during the day; and if a proper degree of moisture is applied, say a light sprinkling once a week, if there is life in the seed, germination is certain. As soon as the seeds have grown so as to attain the first true leaves, (that is, the first leaves that show after the seed-leaves,) they must be "pricked off" carefully in soft, light soil, similar to that used for the seeds, at from one to two inches apart, according to the kind. This will not only prevent them from damping off, as many of them are very apt to do, but they will be much stronger and suffer less when put into flower pots or replanted in the open ground. We prefer to replant the seedlings in the shallow boxes already described. And here we again find, that if the soil is mixed with half its bulk of sifted Cocoanut fiber or Sphagnum, we get a far better development of fibrous roots. They are more portable if planted in boxes than if planted in the soil of the hot-bed, or bench of the green-house, though, of course, after planting in the boxes these are put again in the hot-bed or green-house. After the seedlings have been planted in these boxes, lightly water them and shade for two or three days.

To such as have not the convenience of a hot-bed or green-house, vegetable or flower seeds may be sown in the shallow boxes above mentioned, and placed in the window of a south or east room, where the thermometer does not average less than 70°. Success would be more complete, however, if panes of glass were placed over the seeds, resting on the edge of the box an inch or so from the soil. This would prevent evaporation, and render watering less necessary, and hence less liability to wash up the seeds. With very small seeds it is a good plan to place a sheet of blotting-paper over the boxes after the seeds are sown, and pour the water on the blotting-paper until it soaks through sufficiently to dampen the soil.

ESSAY

ON

ROSE GROWING IN WINTER.

BY PETER HENDERSON.

(Read before the New York Horticultural Society in 1881, with some additions and alterations made in 1883.)

THE intense interest now so generally taken in the culture of the Rose, not only for outside decoration, but for the production of Rose buds in winter, has induced me to attempt a detailed account of the methods of cultivation practised in the vicinity of New York City, which is believed to be unequaled in any other part of the world, particularly in the methods in use for the *winter forcing of the Rose.* For this purpose, strong, healthy cuttings are put in to root at any time from September to January. We keep the sand in our cutting benches about 65 or 70 degrees Fahr., with the temperature of the house 10 degrees less. Rose cuttings, under these conditions, will root in from twenty to twenty-five days, and are then potted in any good soil in two and a half inch pots, and placed in a green-house having a night temperature of about 55 degrees, with 10 to 15 degrees more in the daytime. (See article on *Propagation of Plants*, p. 75.)

The young Roses are regularly shifted into larger pots as soon as the "ball" gets filled with roots, great care being taken that the plants at no time get pot bound.

Syringing is done once a day to keep down red spider, and fumigating by burning tobacco stems to kill the Aphis or Green Fly must be done twice a week. With such attention, plants which were put in as cuttings at the season named above, by the middle of July will be from one and a half to two feet in height,·with roots enough to fill a six-inch pot. They should at this date, or before, be placed out of doors, and stood on rough gravel or cinders, so as to make certain of free drainage.

Now, if intended to be grown in pots, the shifting into larger pots should be repeated whenever the ball gets filled with roots, (which is usually in about five or six weeks after every shift,) until the 1st of October, when they will have reached a size requiring a pot of eight or nine inches in diameter. These pots should be amply drained with broken pots or charcoal, using soil composed of three parts decomposed sod from a good loamy soil to one of well-rotted cow manure, or the soil hereafter advised for benches will do equally well. They are then in condition for winter forcing, no further shifting being required. But if they are to be planted out on benches, or in solid best of soil, the planting should be made from the pots from the 15th of July to the 15th of August.

SOLID BEDS AND RAISED BENCHES.

There is quite a difference of opinion as to whether Roses can be best grown in solid beds or on raised benches. We believe that it really makes but little difference, as we find them grown with nearly equal success by both methods where drainage is perfect, although the method mainly in use at Madison, N. J., where, at present writing, Roses are probably grown better than anywhere else in the country, is the raised bench system. The green-houses used are about twenty feet wide, and are what is known as three-quarter span ; that is, three-quarters of the glass roof slope to the south at an angle of about thirty degrees, while the other quarter slopes north at an angle of twenty degrees, (see Fig. 5, p. 103,) giving a base space for the benches on which the Roses are to be planted, (taking out the walks,) of about fifteen feet. The benches may be either a level platform, or divided into four or five platforms about three feet wide, or so as to be about equal distances from the glass ; the bottom of the benches may be from three, four, or five to six feet from the glass, as desired. There is no necessity for bottom heat for Roses, so that it is best to have the pipes for heating run under the front and back benches of the Rose house, with none under the middle benches.

Soil and Benches.

The soil in which the Roses are to be grown should not be more than five inches deep, the boards being so arranged as to allow free drainage for the water. Perhaps the best way to make the bottom of the bench is to use wall strips or other boards, not to exceed six inches wide, leaving a space of at least half an inch between the boards or strips, so as to make certain of perfect drainage. The bottom is first covered with thin sods, grass side down, and then the soil is placed on to the depth of five inches. This soil is made from sods cut three or four inches thick from any good, loamy pasture land, well chopped up, and mixed with about *one-thirtieth* of their bulk of pure broken bones and bone dust, or *one-third* of well-rotted cow dung to two-thirds of sods, as may be most convenient. In our own practice we use the cow manure in preference to bone dust. It is perhaps best to let the sod be well-rotted before being used, although, if this be not convenient, it will do fresh, if well chopped up.

Distance to Plant.

The distance for Roses such as I describe, (those that have been grown in six-inch pots, and averaging twenty inches high,) should be one foot each way, so as to get the full benefit of a crop by January. It is true that, if planted twice that distance, they would be thick enough before spring; but they would not fill up sufficiently until the middle of January, if planted much wider than one foot. The temperature at which Roses are grown in winter is an average of 55 to 60 degrees at night, with 10 to 15 degrees higher during the day.

Watering and Mulching.

Watering is a matter of the first importance, and requires some experience to know what is the proper condition. As a guide, whenever the soil shows indications of being dry on the top, a thorough watering should be given, sufficient to completely saturate the soil. Such a watering will not usually be required more than once in two weeks. Syringing may be done once a day, sufficient only to moisten the foliage, and often this will be all the watering the Roses require, as getting the soil too wet is certain to destroy the crop. Better to err on the side of dryness, particularly from October to March. Whenever there are indications of the soil being too wet stop syringing, but keep the air of the house moist by watering the paths. Three or four inches of well-rotted cow manure may be used to great advantage as a mulch, put on about the 1st of September, and again about March, as by that time that put on in September will have become exhausted. Fumigating with tobacco smoke for the suppression of the Aphis, (Green Fly,) should be done twice a week; or, what will answer equally well, a mulch of two or three inches of tobacco stems will keep off the Green Fly for five or six weeks.

VARIETIES TO FORCE.

The varieties grown are changing every season, and no list we can give to-day is likely to remain as the best ten years hence. The favorite Tea Roses now grown for winter are *Perle des Jardins*, (yellow,) *Niphetos*, (white,) *Catherine Mermet*, (rosy pink,) *Souvenir d'un Ami*, (delicate peach color,) *Cornelia Cook*, (white,) *Marshal Robert*, (pale yellow,) *Belle Allemande*, (pink,) *Bon Silene*, (carmine,) and *Andrew Schwartz*, (violet crimson.)

There are still a number of the older sorts, such as *Safrano*, *Douglas*, and *Isabella Sprunt*, yet grown; but they are fast giving way to what are known as "fancy" Roses, of which the yellow variety, *Perle des Jardins*, is a type. A new sort, named

SUNSET,

a "sport" from *Perle des Jardins*, has just been originated with us. It is identical in every way with that famous Rose, except that its color, instead of being a canary yellow, as in the *Perle des Jardins*, is a beautiful orange shade of saffron, often seen in the shading of our skies at sunset. For this reason I have given it the descriptive name of "Sunset." Whether for forcing in winter or for out-door in summer, "Sunset" will prove to be one of the most valuable Roses ever introduced. Of Climbing Roses, which are grown on the rafters

NEW TEA ROSE "SUNSET."

of the green-house, *Marshal Niel*, (yellow,) *Lamarque*, (white,) *James Sprunt*, (crimson,) *Gloire de Dijon*, (salmon rose,) and *Red Gloire de Dijon*, (carmine,) are the best.

Another class of Roses, the Hybrid Perpetuals, particularly the variety known as *General Jacqueminot*, are now grown in immense quantities. These, we think, may soon be supplanted by a newer class, known as " Hybrid

Teas," of which *Duchess of Edinburgh*, (bright crimson,) *La France*, (light pink,) *Duke of Connaught*, (crimson scarlet,) *Duchess of Connaught*, (deep carmine,) *Coquette des Alpes*, (white,) *Her Majesty*, (blush,) and *Wm. Henry Bennett*, (crimson,) are at present types. These require an entirely different treatment from the Tea Roses proper, as they are not strictly evergreens, but partly drop their leaves in the fall; and hence, like all deciduous plants, require a rest of at least two months, either by drying or by a low temperature, before they can be forced into flower, so as to produce the best results.

FORCING HYBRID PERPETUALS AND HYBRID TEAS.

To get the Hybrid Perpetual and the Hybrid Tea classes early, (say during January,) requires special skill and care, but well repays the trouble, as this class of Roses now bring an average of $50 per hundred buds at wholesale from the 15th of December to January 15th. The method found to be necessary is to grow these Roses on in pots, exactly as recommended for the evergreen or Tea Roses, except that, as they have a tendency to grow tall, the center should be pinched out of the leading shoots, so that from five to six shoots run up, and thus not only make the plant bushy, but, what is of more importance, these slimmer shoots are less pithy and ripen off harder, thus insuring with more certainty a greater production of buds.

The plants, if started from cuttings any time from September to January, which is the season we prefer to root them in, will, if properly grown, by August 1st, (or at less than one year old,) have filled a seven or eight inch pot with roots. Now is the critical point. The plants must be ripened off and rested, if a crop of buds is wanted by January and February; so, to do this at a season as early as the 1st of August, the plants must be gradually dried off sufficiently to make them drop their leaves, though not to so violently wilt them as to shrivel the shoots. A rest of two months is necessary, so that the plants begun to be dried off by the 1st of August may be started slowly by the 1st of October, and those begun to be dried off by the 1st of September may be started, also at as low a temperature as possible, by the 1st of November. These, like the Monthly Roses, are best ripened off by placing them in the open air; though, if continued wet weather occur when they are thus placed to dry and ripen their wood, the pots must be placed on their sides, or some arrangement contrived to keep them from getting wet, otherwise the rest absolutely necessary for early forcing cannot be obtained.

When the forcing of General Jacqueminot or other Hybrid Perpetual Roses is successful, it is very profitable. Why it is profitable is from the fact of unusual care and skill being required to have the plants in the proper condition. We may here state that many failures have resulted from the attempt to grow the Hybrid Tea Roses without resting, notably the *Duchess of Edinburgh*, which was sent out from England some five or six years ago as a "Crimson Tea." The misleading name of "Tea" induced hundreds of florists to attempt its growth under the same conditions as the *Safrano* or *Bon Silene* class, and the consequence was in every case almost complete failure. This type evidently partakes more of the Hybrid Perpetual than of the Tea class, and as they are hardy and deciduous, refuse to blossom in midwinter, unless given the rest that their nature demands.

Mildew.

Roses, when grown under glass, with proper attention to temperature and moisture, are not usually attacked by mildew; but as a preventive it is well to paint the hot-water pipes once every two or three weeks with a mixture of sulphur and lime or sulphur and guano, made of the consistency of whitewash, (the guano or lime is merely to make the sulphur stick better to the pipes.) The fumes of sulphur, as diffused by the heated pipes, is a never-failing means of destroying the germs of mildew or any other fungoid growth, and also holds in check, to some extent, the Red Spider insect, often so troublesome to the Rose.

Rose Bug.

For the Rose Bug, so destructive to success in Rose growing under glass, there seems no remedy except the slow and unsatisfactory one of catching and killing the insect as soon as it is seen on the leaves. It is not easily observed, as it gets under the leaves and close to the shoots of the plants. Its presence is known by the bitten leaves showing where it is feeding; but even with the greatest diligence enough will usually escape to deposit their eggs in the soil, which, when hatched out to the grub or pupa state, rapidly begin the work of destruction by feeding on the roots. In this stage, all attempts to destroy them have thus far, I believe, failed.

The only safety, when the Rose Bug is known to be present in sufficient numbers to injure, is to throw out the plants and start with young ones. I have, for three years past, adopted the plan of growing the plants only one year old from cuttings rooted during the fall or winter months, and have since then had no trouble whatever from the ravages of this insect. I know, of course, that there are many Rose houses that are even nine to ten years old, that never fail to produce abundant crops, particularly such as Marshal Niel and other climbers; but in such cases it seems to be that the Roses planted either had escaped the visitation of the Rose Bug altogether, or had got so deeply and strongly rooted before being attacked that the grub could not injure the plants.

SHADING THE HOUSE.

There is some difference of opinion as to the propriety of shading Rose houses during the hot summer months. I believe that a slight shading is beneficial from May to September, and for that purpose use naphtha, mixed with a little white lead, just enough to give it the appearance of thin milk. This is thrown on the outside of the glass with a syringe. It costs only about twenty-five cents for every thousand square feet. This shading is the best I have ever used. It is just enough to take the glare of the sunlight off, without much lessening the light; and though it will hold on tenaciously during the summer, it is easily rubbed off in the fall after the first frost.

GARDEN CULTURE OF THE ROSE.

But little need be said on this branch of the subject, all that is wanted being a deep, rich soil, in an unshaded position. For the dry climate of the United States, a class of Roses should be grown very different from those grown in England. There the "Remontants," or "Hybrid Perpetuals," in the humid atmosphere that prevails, with few exceptions flower nearly as freely as the "Monthly" Roses do here; but with us, experience has shown that, after the first bloom in June, no full crop of flowers is again obtained, unless with the comparatively new class known as the Hybrid Teas, of which "La France" and "Duchess of Edinburgh" are types; so that, when a continued bloom of Roses is desired during the entire summer and fall months, the class known as monthly (embracing Tea, Bourbon, Bengal, Noisette, and Hybrid Tea) are the best. True, these varieties, except the "Hybrid Teas," are not usually hardy, unless in that portion of the country where the thermometer never gets 20° below the freezing point; but they can be saved through the winter in almost any section, if pegged down and covered up with five or six inches of leaves or rough litter. This covering, however, should not be done until quite hard frost comes; in the locality of New York, about the first week in December. If done sooner, there is danger, if the season is mild, (as it usually is here until December 1st), that the shoots may be smothered and decay by a too early covering. This same rule I adopt in covering Grape Vines, Clematis, Raspberries, Strawberries, or, in fact, any other plant or shrub that I believe to be benefited by winter protection, as I have never yet seen injury done to half-hardy plants by frost previous to that date. In this matter of covering, the amateur in gardening often errs; first, from his anxiety to protect his plants before there is danger in the fall; and next, in his enthusiasm in spring, he is deceived by some warm day in March to uncover what is not safe until April.

Rose Buds in Summer.

The great want of fine Rose buds during the summer months induced me, last season, to adopt a method that promises great success. In August strong plants were set out in cold frames, (such as are used for keeping Cabbage, Pansies, or other half-hardy plants,) at a distance of one foot each way. On the approach of cold weather in November they were mulched with two or three inches of dry leaves, and by the time the thermometer began to fall to $10°$ or $15°$ below the freezing point, the sashes were put on, care being taken to give ventilation, so as to keep them cool. They thus become hardened enough to go safely through the winter. By the middle of April the sashes may be left entirely off, provided care has been taken to keep them cool throughout the winter. Roses being thus "rested," (which is the great necessity for the best results in Rose culture,) an abundant crop of buds may be expected from June to October, provided that proper attention has been given to watering and mulching with well-rotted stable manure, or moss and bone dust. This mulching should take the place of the dry leaves (which were placed on in the fall) about the latter end of May or first of June.

The Roses to be used for summer buds must be all full, double flowers, else they will quickly fall to pieces in hot weather. Such kinds as Safrano, Bon Silene, and Douglas, are of no use for this purpose. The kinds we have used are as follows: *Perle des Jardins*, (yellow,) *Cornelia Cook*, (white,) *La France*, (light rose,) *Coquette des Alpes*, (pure white,) *Madame Welch*, (blush,) *Duchess of Edinburgh*, (crimson,) *Malmaison*, (deep blush,) *Catherine Mermet*, (rosy pink,) *Letty Coles*, (carmine and blush,) *Devoniensis*, (deep blush,) and *Sunset*, (the new orange saffron variety,) all of which, under proper conditions, will give perfect flowers in the hottest weather.

GREEN-HOUSE STRUCTURES,

AND

MODES OF HEATING.

The construction of green-houses is now a matter of much interest to a large portion of the community. I have many applications every season from florists, private gentlemen, and market gardeners, asking me which is the best way to build this and that kind of a green-house. I find it practically impossible to intelligently reply to all these inquiries by letter, and have for this reason written this article, giving such information

FIGURE 1. (Scale ⅙ of an inch to the foot.)

as I possess on the most approved methods of construction and heating up to the present time.

When a green-house of any large extent for private use is to be constructed, involving an amount of, say $5,000 and upward, I always recommend it to be the cheapest plan to get the advice of a professional green-house architect on the subject; but as a great many parties wish to build only small green-houses for private purposes, doubtless to such my experience may be of interest and value. The scale used in all the plans throughout is one-eighth of an inch to the foot.

For a small green-house, that shown by Figure 1, having a curvilinear roof, is a convenient and desirable form, the dimensions being 20 feet wide by 50 feet

FIGURE 2. (Scale ⅛ of an inch to the foot.)

long. Figure 1 is the end elevation. Figure 2 is a section, showing the inside view of walk, benches, and heating-pipes.

It is often desirable to attach a green-house or conservatory to the dwelling-house. That shown by Figure 3 has a width of 12 feet, though, of course, the width or length is a matter of taste or convenience. If the greenhouse is wanted for commercial use, what the particular use is must be determined before beginning to build. If for the general purpose of growing bedding plants, then

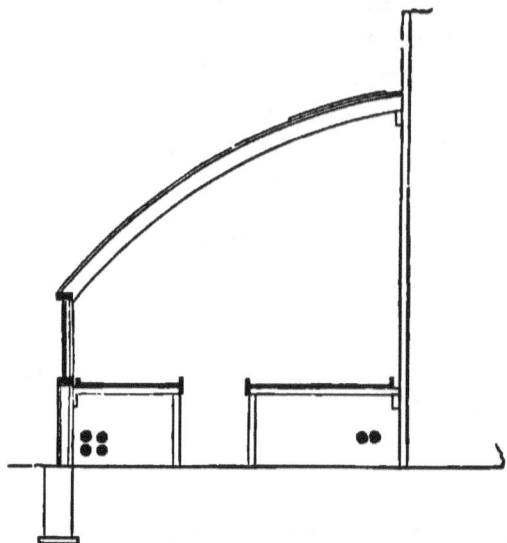

FIGURE 3. (Scale ⅛ of an inch to the foot.)

nothing, we think, is better than the style of houses we ourselves use, (Figure 4,) which average 20 feet in width, and are of a uniform length of 100 feet. Of course the length is a matter of convenience, but the width we find is an important point to consider ; for if over 20 feet the benches are too wide to reach easily, and if under 20 feet room is lost by the necessity of having two walks in a narrow space. Figure 4 shows the inside arrangement of this style of green-house as we have it in use. One section shows a bench in the middle, the other a solid bed of soil. The scale (one-eighth of an inch to the foot) will give the height of the wall, benches, etc.

These green-houses are joined together on the ridge and furrow plan, having one slope to the west and the other slope to the east; but if wanted for the purpose of

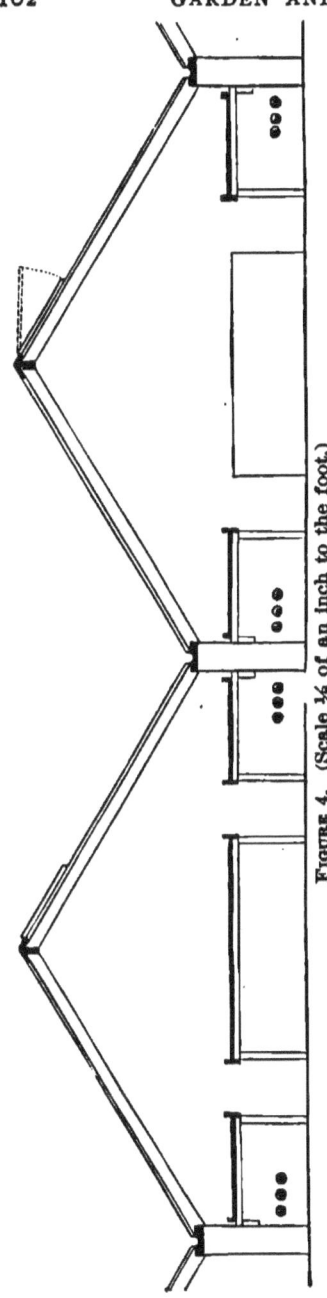

FIGURE 4. (Scale ⅙ of an inch to the foot.)

growing rose-buds in winter, or, in short, for almost any kind of plants grown for the flowers during the winter months, this style of greenhouse (that shown by Figure 4) is not suited, as it is found that, when joined on the ridge and furrow plan, there is too much shadow, and the necessary light required for the best development of flowers in winter is not admitted, so that I now find that for all kinds of flowering plants, Roses particularly, the green-house structure should stand alone, and be of the style known as the three-quarter span; that is, having an angle of about 32 degrees to the horizon to the south, and an angle of 36 or 38 degrees to the north, as shown by Figure 5, which is on the same scale.

For the same reason, (the necessity of sunlight in winter,) the wood work should be made as light as possible consistent with strength, and for this purpose I prefer to use well-seasoned yellow pine, as it has more strength, in proportion to bulk, than white pine. It is also necessary to use glass not less than 10 × 12, put in the 12 way. This style of green-house is now preferred for forcing Lettuce, Strawberries, and other fruits and

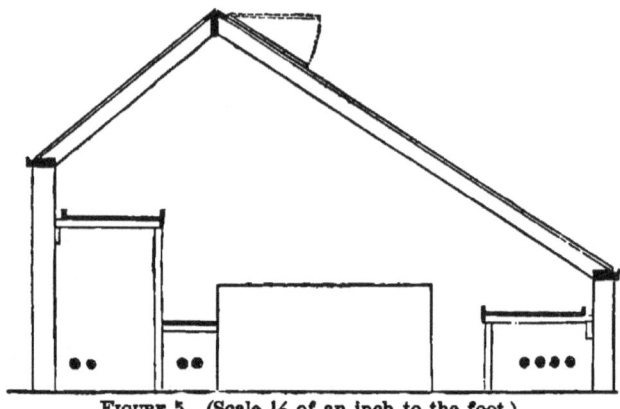

FIGURE 5. (Scale ⅛ of an inch to the foot.)

vegetables in winter, as well as flowering plants, as they too require all the light that it is possible to obtain.

Although this style of green-house would also shade, if joined together on the ridge and furrow plan, when built on level ground, yet, whenever a convenient location can be had, where the ground slopes to the south at an angle of 10 or 15 degrees, they may be joined together as seen in Figure 6, (one-eighth of an inch to the foot scale,) which shows a slope or angle of 15 degrees.

It will be noticed in this design (Figure 6) that the larger number of pipes are placed under the front bench, there being four there, while there are only two under the back bench. The slope of the ground makes this arrangement necessary in order to secure an equal distribution of heat. With the ordinary arrangement of pipes, (half under each bench,) the back of the house would always be much the warmest, as a moment's reflection

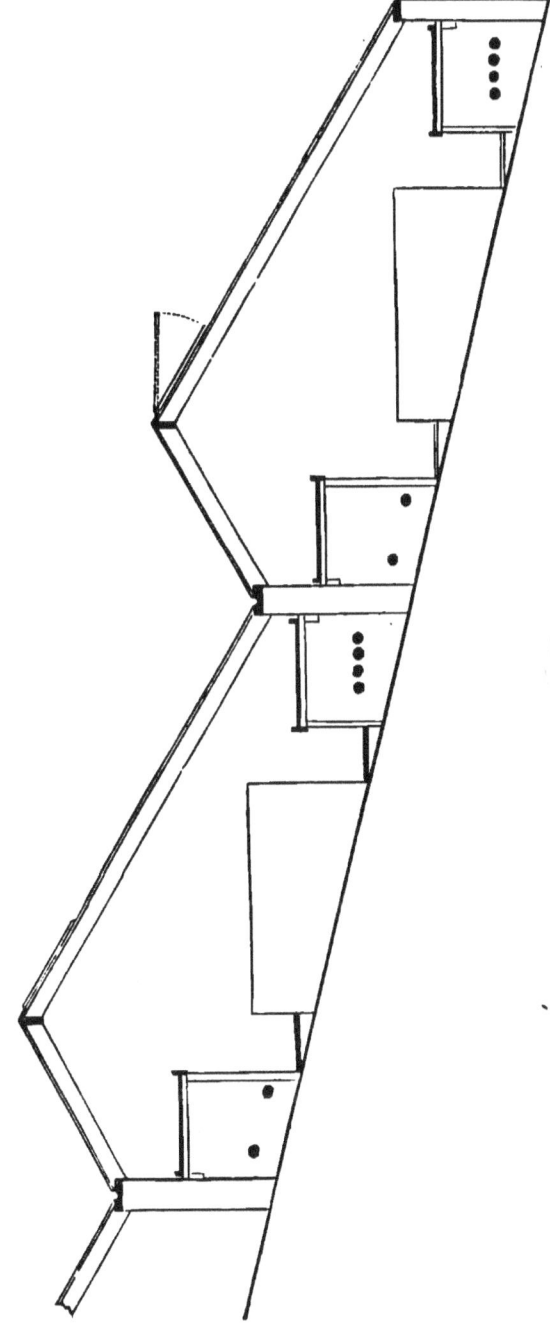

FIGURE 6. (Scale ⅛ of an inch to the foot.)

will make manifest. The position of the ventilators near the ridge is distinctly marked in this and all the other figures, the dotted lines showing a ventilator raised or open. The position of the benches is also shown. Through the middle there may be either a bench or a solid bed of earth. By use of the scale (one eighth of an inch to the foot) the proportions of the details of this house may be readily obtained.

The construction of green-houses for private purposes is often very costly and elaborate, the foundation being formed of concrete, stone, or brick ; but after the wall has risen to the surface of the ground, it is found that, unless the wall of stone or brick is very thick indeed, the high temperature and moisture inside of a green-house soon injures the mason work by warring with the low temperature outside, particularly on the north or northwest side. For this reason it has been found that wooden walls, for ordinary purposes, are equally as good as an eight-inch brick wall for resisting cold, far cheaper, and more durable.

A common error with the inexperienced is to build the wooden wall of a green-house hollow, filling up the space with sawdust, or some such non-conducting material. The method found best is to sink locust, cedar, or chestnut posts to the required depth, and at distances of four or six feet apart ; against these (outside) nail common rough boards ; then against these tack asphalt or tarred paper, and against that nail the ordinary weather boarding. Such a wall will resist cold better than an eight-inch brick wall, and will last for twenty years if kept painted. If a better finish is desired inside, the posts can be hid by weather boarding ; but nothing should be put in to fill the space. When the walls have been finished to the required height, the wall plate to secure the rafters is laid on. Supporting posts should be placed under the ridge pole, and also near the middle of the rafters, where these are very long, as is the case in many of the three-quarter span houses.

Glass and Glazing.

If for winter forcing of either fruit or flowers, the glass should (as we have before said) be not less than 10 × 12 in size, and laid in the 12 way. It should be of what is known as second quality French, and it is economy always to use the double thick. All panes should be rejected having flaws or lenses, else these will form a focus for the sun's rays and burn the leaves of the plants ; but even with the greatest care, some flaws will usually remain, and less or more burn the leaves after the sun becomes strong, to counteract which a slight shading had better be used on the glass from April to September. We use naphtha, with just enough white lead mixed in it to give it the appearance of thin milk. This we put on with a syringe, which sufficiently covers up all flaws in the glass to prevent burning, and at the same time tends to cool the house from the violence of the sun's rays. This is by far the cheapest and best shading we have ever used. It can be gradated to any degree of thickness, and costs only about 25 cents per 1,000 square feet of glass, for material and labor.

In glazing, the method now almost universally adopted is to bed the glass in putty, and tack it on top with glazier's points, using no putty on the top. The glazier's points are triangular, one corner of which is turned down, so that when it is driven in, it fits the lower edge of each pane and prevents it from slipping down. A great mistake is often made in giving the glass too much lap;

it should only be given just enough to cover the edge of the pane, (from one-eighth to one-fourth of an inch.) If given too much, the water gets in, and when it freezes it cracks the glass.

Ground Glass.

The use of ground glass is gradually becoming greater every season. I confess to having had a prejudice against it, thinking that it obscured the sun's rays too much, and was apprehensive that, for that reason, it would not be so well suited for plants in winter; but from an examination last season of a large lot of green-houses glazed with such glass, and used for various purposes, I am convinced that it obscures the light only in a very small degree, if at all; for in the green-houses referred to, plants of all descriptions, both for foliage and for fruit, as well as for producing flowers in winter, were under culture, and they could not have been in better condition than they were. The advantage of the ground glass is, that it entirely prevents the burning of the foliage, which is a source of great annoyance in the cultivation of plants and fruits. I am so convinced of the utility of it, that whenever I again construct more green-houses for my own use I shall use it. It costs but little more than the glass in common use, and must be a great saving, as it does away with the necessity for shading during the summer months, shading being mainly used to prevent the burning or blistering of the leaves.

Heating by Hot Water.

The mode of heating in general use is by hot water, though many beginners with limited means still use smoke flues. In heating by hot water it is important that the work be given to some reputable firm, whose knowledge is such as will enable them not only to judge what is the proper capacity of the boiler for the number of pipes to be used, but also how many pipes are necessary to be used for the surface of glass to be heated. Men who have done a large business in heating green-houses have far better opportunities for knowledge in this matter than the average gardener or florist; and if those erecting green-houses have not had extensive and varied practice, they had better be guided by the men who make a business of heating, as the want of the requisite knowledge of these matters often works serious mischief. Of course, the size of the green-house or green-houses to be heated must determine the capacity of the boiler wanted; but the boiler being properly apportioned to the length of pipe, the following data, used in our own establishment, may be useful. In our houses, which are 20 feet wide and 100 feet long, when a night temperature of 70° is required in the coldest weather, ten runs or rows of four-inch pipe, five on each side; when 60° are wanted, eight runs of pipe, four on each side; when 50° are wanted, six runs of pipe; and when only 35° or 40° are wanted, four runs of pipe. This is for the latitude of New York city, where the temperature rarely falls lower than 10° below zero. Latitudes north or south of New York should be graded accordingly. If estimated by glass surface, about one foot in length of four-inch pipe is necessary for every three and a half square feet of glass surface, when the temperature is at 10° below zero, to keep a temperature of 50° in the green-house. We now place all our pipes under the side benches, as that enables us to use the space under the middle for stowing away many plants safely, which otherwise could not be done if the pipes were there. There are scores of kinds of hot-water boilers in use, and our opinion is repeatedly asked as to the relative merits of many of them. This can only be determined by a comparative test, which we have never had time or inclination to try. We have used the boilers made by Hitchings & Co. for the past twenty years with the most satisfactory results. There may be better, but we do not know it, and do not care to take the risk of experimenting.

Heating by Flues.

For beginners with small means, when personal attention can be given to the fires, by heating green-houses with flues a great saving in cost can be made; in fact, nearly half the cost of construction; for we find that the hot-water heating apparatus usually is half the cost of ordinary commercial green-houses, while if heated by flues the cost would not be more than ten per cent. of the whole. A new method of constructing flues, (or rather a revived method, for it originated in 1822,) has been in use for the past few years, which has such manifest advantages that many now use it who would no doubt otherwise have used hot-water heating. Its peculiarity consists in running the flue back to the furnace from which it starts and into the chimney, which is built on the top of the furnace. As soon as the fire is lighted in the furnace, the brick-work forming the arch gets heated, and at once starts an upward draft, driving out the cold air from the chimney, which puts the smoke flue into immediate action and maintains it; hence there is never any trouble about the draft, as in ordinary flues having the chimney at the most distant point from the furnace.

By this plan we not only get rid of the violent heat given out by the furnace, but at the same time it insures

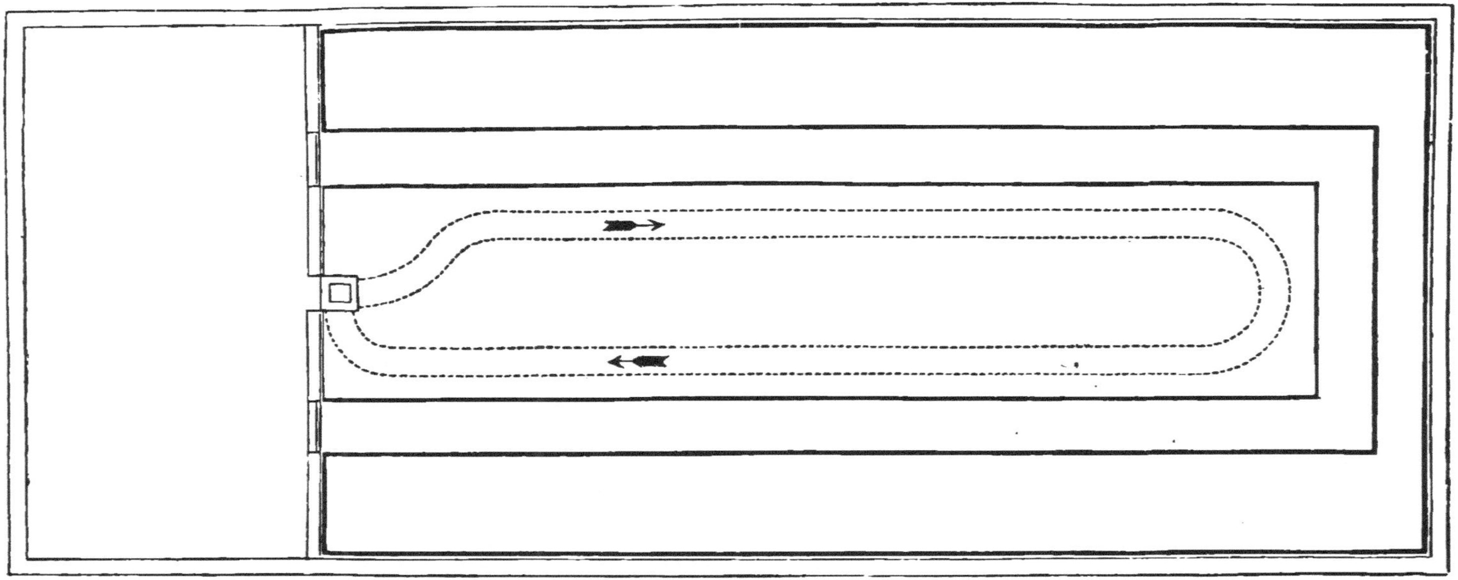

FIGURE 7. (Scale ½ of an inch to the foot.)

a complete draft, so that the heated air from the furnace is so rapidly carried through the entire length of the flue, that it is nearly as hot when it enters the chimney as when it left the furnace. This perfect draft also does away with all danger of the escape of gas from the flues into the green-house, which often happens when the draft is not active. Although no system of heating by smoke flues is so satisfactory as by hot water, yet there are hundreds who have neither the means nor the inclination to go to the greater expense of hot-water heating, and to such this revived method is one that will, to a great extent, simplify and cheapen the erection of greenhouses. Many old-established florists, who have had the old plan of flues in use, have changed them to the one here described, and with great satisfaction. The wonder is that such an important fact has been so long overlooked, for at the time it was discovered heating greenhouses by flues was almost the only method in use.

Figure 7 (one-eighth of an inch to the foot scale) shows a green-house 20 feet wide by 50 feet long, with furnace room, or shed, 10 × 20 feet. Here the flues are so disposed as to avoid crossing the walks, being placed under the center bench, but as near as possible to the walk on each side, so that the heat may be evenly diffused throughout. If a difference in temperature is required in a house of this kind, it may be obtained by running a glass partition *across* the house, say at 25 feet from the furnace end, which will, of course, make the latter end the hottest. It will be observed that the plan (Figure 7) shows by dotted lines this new or revived plan of flue heating. Figure 8 (the same scale) is a section, showing the arrangement of the benches, etc.

In constructing the furnace for flue heating, the size of the furnace doors should be, for a green-house 20 × 50, about 14 inches square, and the length of the furnace bars 30 inches; the furnace should be arched over, and the top of the inside of the arch should be about 20 inches from the bars. The flue will always "draw" better if slightly on the ascent throughout its entire

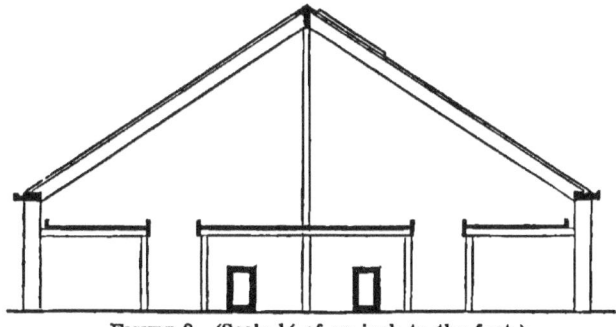

FIGURE 8. (Scale ⅙ of an inch to the foot.)

length. It should be elevated in all cases from the ground, on flags or bricks, so that its heat may be given out on all sides. The inside measure of the brick flue should not be less than 8 × 14 inches. If tiles can be conveniently procured, they are best to cover with; but, if not, the top of the flue may be contracted to six inches, and covered with bricks.

After the flue has been built of brick to twenty-five or thirty feet from the furnace, cement or vitrified drain pipe, eight or nine inches in diameter, should be used, as they are not only cheaper, but radiate the heat quicker than the bricks; they are also much easier constructed and cleaned. Care should be taken that no woodwork is in contact with the flue at any place. It should be taken as a safe rule, that woodwork should in no case be nearer the flue or furnace than eight inches. In constructing, do not be influenced by what the mechanics will tell you, as few of them have any experience in such matters, and are not able to judge of the dangers resulting from woodwork being in close contact with the heated bricks. (For cost of construction see page 116.)

Heating by Steam.

Steam heating, we think, in all probability will soon be extensively used, particularly in large establishments that are put up at one time. The following is from E. H. Bochman, Pittsburgh, Penn., who has been eminently successful with steam heating for green-houses. He is strong in the belief that it will eventually supersede all other methods. He says:

"*The New System of Heating Green-houses by Low-pressure Steam*, by which are gained important advantages in every essential requisite in a heating apparatus, viz., *efficiency, economy* of fuel and attention, *safety*, and *simplicity*, consists of a series of steam tubes of *not less than two inches in diameter*, placed under the benches or suspended along the walls, as may be best suited, in such a manner as to drain themselves into a water and steam-tight vessel, which, therefore, has to be situated at the lowest convenient point. These tubes or pipes should present a radiating surface of about one square foot to ten square feet of glass surface; or, better expressed, one square foot to seventy cubic feet of space to be heated to at least 55° in any weather up, or rather down to 25° below zero, and at a pressure of steam *not to exceed fifteen pounds* to the square inch. If a higher temperature is desired, say from 65° to 70°, make the radiating surface equal, say, one square foot to fifty cubic feet for the same pressure of steam. The *form* of *boiler* is *immaterial;* whichever is best suited and most economical for the particular fuel you use, is the one to adopt, and its capacity should *not be less* than one horse power to 120 square feet of radiating surface, which, represented in two-inch pipe, is, in round numbers, 240 lineal feet. This boiler should be provided with an *automatic* and *positive-acting steam trap*, to return the condensation which gathers in the vessel above mentioned to the boiler, *thereby maintaining at all times sufficient water;* in fact, establishing complete circulation, much the same as by hot water; and when you add to this an efficient *automatic damper-regulator*, (do not let yourself be humbugged into any diaphragm nuisance,) you have ' *The coming heating apparatus*,' compared to which any other hitherto in use, of whatever form, is a cumbersome, wasteful, and inefficient affair. Five seasons' use speaks volumes for its superiority, and it has already the entire endorsement of some of the most successful and progressive commercial florists of the country."

HEATING BY HOT-BEDS.
(From Henderson's Hand-Book of Plants.)

The preparation of the heating material for the hot-bed is a matter of importance. It should be manure fresh from the horse-stable, and when they can be procured, it is better to mix it with about an equal bulk of leaves from the woods, or refuse hops. If the weather is very cold, the bulk of manure must be of good size, from five to six wagon loads, thrown into a compact round heap, else the mass may be so chilled that heat will not generate. If a shed is convenient, the manure may be placed there, especially if the quantity is small, to be protected from cold until the heat begins to rise. The heap should be turned and well broken up before being used for the hot-beds, so that the rank steam may escape, and the manure become of the proper " sweetened " condition. It is economy of the heating material to use a pit for the hot-bed. This should be made from two to three feet deep, six feet wide, and of any required length.

After the heating material has been packed in the pit to the depth of twenty to twenty-four inches, according to the purpose for which it is wanted, or the season of the year, (the earlier in the season, the deeper it is needed,) the sashes should be placed on the frame, and kept close until the heat generates in the hot-bed, which will usually take twenty-four hours. Now plunge a thermometer into the manure, and if all is right it will indicate 100 degrees or more ; but this is yet too hot as bottom heat for the growth of seeds or plants, and a few days of delay must be allowed until the thermometer indicates a falling of 8 or 10 degrees, when four or five inches of soil may be placed upon the manure, and the seeds sown or plants set out in the hot-bed. Amateurs are apt to be impatient in the matter of hot-beds, and often lose their first crop by sowing or planting before the first violent heat has subsided. Another very common mistake is in beginning too early in the season. In the latitude of New York nothing is gained by beginning before the first week in March, and the result will be very nearly as good if not begun until a month later.

There are two or three important matters to bear in mind in the use of hot-beds. It is indispensable for safety to cover the glass at night with shutters or mats until all danger of frost is over ; for it must be remembered that the contents of a hot-bed are always tender, from being forced so rapidly by the heat below, and that the slightest frost will kill them. Again, there is danger of overheating in the daytime by a neglect to ventilate when the sun is shining. As a general rule, it will be safe in all the average days of March, April, and May, to have the sash of the hot-bed tilted up from an inch to three inches at the back from 9 A. M. to 4 P. M. Much will, of course, depend upon the activity of the heating material in the hot-bed, the warmth of the weather, and the character of the plants in the bed, so that we can only give a loose general rule. Numbers of inexperienced amateur cultivators often lose the entire contents of their hot-beds by having omitted to ventilate them, and on their return home from business at night find all the contents scorched up ; or the danger of the other extreme is, that the plants are frozen through neglect to cover them at night. A hot-bed requires a certain amount of attention, which must be given at the right time, or no satisfactory results can be expected.

Cost of Construction.

Estimates of the cost of green-houses must necessarily be only approximate, according as to how the work is done, when done, and the ever-changing cost of material and labor. In this vicinity, at this time, a green-house 20 × 100 would cost about $12 per running foot. If two together, (ridge and furrow, as in Figure 4,) each 20 × 50, about $10 per running foot for each house. A green-house like Figure 3, attached to a dwelling, would cost about $10 per running foot; and one 20 × 50, like Figures 1 and 2, (curved roof and double pitch,) would cost proportionately. (These estimates do *not* include heating.) Heating by hot water would cost about two-thirds more, making the cost complete about $1,650. If heated by flues, as in Figures 7 and 8, only about two per cent. more would be required, or say about $1,100 complete.

FORMATION

AND

RENOVATION OF LAWNS.

BY PETER HENDERSON.

(Read before the National Convention of Nurserymen, Florists, and Seedsmen, held at St. Louis, Mo., June 20th, 1883.)

WE not unfrequently see, after a dwelling costing $5,000, $10,000, $20,000, or $30,000 is erected, that the grounds surrounding it are left to the tender mercy of some ignorant pretender to grade and put in shape. The educated, intelligent architect's duties in many cases end with the completion of the building, and the "garden architect" (likely some pretentious laborer) is installed to grade for the lawn; and a common consequence is, that the beauty of the place may be forever marred; for this matter really in many cases requires as much intelligence and good judgment as the construction of the dwelling itself.

DRAINING AND GRADING.

One of the first conditions for a perfect lawn is, that the land be perfectly drained either naturally or artificially. If the subsoil is sand or gravel, so that water can quickly pass through it, then there will be no need for artificial drains; but if there is a stratum of adhesive clay for a subsoil, then drains are indispensable every fifteen or twenty feet. As the formation of the lawn is the foundation of all subsequent operations, it is imperative that it be carefully done; for if badly done at first it cannot be changed or altered, unless to the great detriment of trees or shrubs that have been planted, or flower beds or walks that have been laid out.

The first thing to be done is to get the ground shaped to the desired grade, taking care, in grading, that when hills or rocks are removed, sufficient subsoil is also removed to be replaced with top soil, so that at least five inches of good soil will overlay the whole in all places; and where trees are to be planted there should be twice that depth of good soil. When the grading is finished, if the nature of the ground requires it, drains should be laid wherever necessary; and then the whole should be thoroughly plowed, a subsoil following in the wake of the common plow, until it is completely pulverized. A heavy harrow should then be applied until the surface is thoroughly fined down. All stones, roots, etc., should be removed, so that a smooth surface may be obtained. We have used, with great effect and saving of labor, a comparatively new implement known as the " Disc Smoothing Harrow," which fines and levels the land equal to a steel rake; and whenever large areas are in preparation for lawns, or, in fact, for any field culture requiring a fine, smooth surface, this implement will be found to be of great value.

SOWING.

When the seed is sown a light harrow snould be again applied, so as to sink the seed two inches or so in the soil, and after that a thorough rolling given, so that the surface is made as smooth and firm as possible. In the latitude of New York, the seed may be sown any time during the months of April and May, and will form a good lawn by July or August if the preparation has been good, or in from *sixty to one hundred days* from the time of sowing. If sown in the hot months of June or July, a sprinkling of oats should be sown at the same time, so that the shade given by the oats will protect the young grass from the sun. Lawns are very often sown during the early fall months (September being the best) with excellent results.

In my extensive experience, I have found that the formula for seed for lawn grass, which I call the "Central Park Mixture," is in all respects the best. On some soils Kentucky Blue Grass is used alone, but for a firm, carpet-like lawn I consider the "Central Park Lawn Mixture" preferable. For small plots, of course, digging, trenching, and raking must be done instead of plowing, subsoiling, and harrowing, and the surface, after sowing, should be patted down with the back of a spade or rolled down with a roller.

Sodding.

In sloping banks it is often necessary to use sod, as the rains wash the soil off before the grass seed has had time to germinate. It is sometimes even necessary, in sodding very steep banks, to use pins eight or ten inches in length to pin the sods in place, to prevent them from being washed down by excessive rains before the grass roots have had time to fasten in the soil. In small yards sodding is often done so as to get immediate results; but in all such cases great care should be taken to see that the sods used are of the proper quality, otherwise it is much better to wait a few months for the lawn seed to produce the lawn.

QUANTITY OF SEED.

As a guide for the proper quantity of seed required to form a perfect lawn, I may state that one quart of " Central Park Lawn Mixture " is sufficient to thoroughly sow an area of 20 feet by 15 feet, (300 square feet;) or, to cover an acre, four bushels will be required. It should be borne in mind that, in order to produce the best results, grass seed for lawns should be sown at least twice as thickly as if sown for hay. In fact, if very rapid results are wanted, a lawn will be much quicker obtained by using twice as much seed per acre. In a lawn of about an acre in extent, which I made this season, eight bushels of "Central Park Mixture" were sown on the 25th of April, harrowed well in with the ordinary farm harrow, and then rolled firmly with a heavy iron roller. The result was, that by July 1st, or about sixty days from the date of sowing, a perfect lawn was obtained, having had to be twice mowed over by a machine previous to that date.

FERTILIZERS FOR THE LAWN.

The question of fertilizers for the lawn is an important one. If the soil is naturally a deep, rich loam, it is not indispensable that manure at all be used the season of sowing, although in every case it would be an advantage, and is really essential if the soil is poor or light. Perhaps the best way to apply well-rotted stable manure, is to spread it thick enough to cover the ground after plowing or digging, and then harrow or rake it in; but when cost is no special object, the best plan to insure permanency for the lawn is to use, as above, from 2,500 to 3,000 pounds of coarse ground bone per acre, or in that proportion for lesser areas, as the bone decomposes slowly. This quantity, harrowed or raked deeply in, would insure a "velvet lawn," under ordinary circumstances, for six or eight years without further application of manures.

Top Dressing.

When the land has not been fertilized before sowing, it is necessary to use some top dressing of manure each season to keep up the fertility of the lawn, and nothing is better for this purpose than to spread over it late in the fall, (November or December,) enough short stable manure to partially cover the surface. This should be allowed to remain on until such times as the grass shows signs of starting in the spring, when the rough portion should be raked off and a heavy roller applied, so that the surface of the lawn may be rendered smooth and firm for the mower. If the top dressing of stable manure has been omitted in the fall, fine bone dust, mixed with finely sifted coal or wood ashes, in equal parts, may be sown on the lawn about as thick as sand is usually strewn on the floor, and rolled down.

Mowing.

Mowing should be begun in the spring as soon as the grass is two or three inches high, and continued every seven or eight days until the cessation of growth in the fall. If the lawn is gone over with the mower once a week, the clippings are best left on, as the sun quickly shrivels them up so that they never appear unsightly; but if mowing is delayed two or three weeks, then the grass must be raked off; and besides the labor of so doing, the rake always more or less injures the lawn during the growing season.

Destroying Weeds.

It sometimes happens that the soil contains seeds of perennial plants. Such seeds are rarely found in the grass seed, such as Dandelion, Dock, or Thistles, but they seriously interfere with the beauty of the lawn. When such occur, there is no other remedy than the slow process of cutting them out with a knife. It is not necessary to take them out by the root; if the "crowns" of these perennial weeds are cut just below the surface, they will not again grow.

Renovating Lawns.

To renovate lawns that have become worn out by neglect or other causes, and where it is not convenient or desirable to renew by plowing up, they may be greatly benefited by running a light harrow over them, if the surface is large, or by a sharp steel rake for smaller areas. After stirring the surface by such means judiciously, so as not to too severely hurt the roots, lawn grass seed should be sown over the surface, using about half the quantity advised for new lawns. After sowing, the surface should be harrowed or raked over, and firmly rolled or beaten down; but if spurious grass or other weeds have got possession of the lawn, then this way of renovation would not be satisfactory, and it had better be plowed under and sown afresh, in the manner already given for the formation of the lawn.

ONION GROWING

for

MARKET.

Soil.

It is the generally received opinion that Onions grow best in old ground. This, I think, is an error. It is not because the ground is "old," or has been long cultivated, that the Onions do better there, but because such lands, from their long culture, are usually better pulverized; and experience has shown me repeatedly, that when new soil has been equally well pulverized and fertilized, an equally good crop is obtained, and usually a cleaner crop, more exempt from rust or mildew. As a matter of fact, the finest crop of Onions I ever beheld was on sandy swamp land, which had been first thoroughly drained and broken up. In fact, new soils, particularly when broken up from pasture land, (turned over early enough in the fall, so that the sod is rotted completely,) make excellent land for Onion crops, as they are usually free from weeds. Such land, however, must be well pulverized by the use of the plow, harrow, and smoothing harrow, or good results may not follow. Much depends on the quality of such soil. If rather sandy loam, it will, of course, be much easier to pulverize than if stiff or clayey loam, and such soil, in my experience, is always preferable for most crops. Such soils, also, are nearly always free from under water, rarely requiring artificial drainage, if the land is level, and it always should be selected as level as possible for the Onion crop, as when land slopes to any great extent, much damage is often done by washing out, the Onion roots being near the surface, and, consequently, cannot resist floods as crops do that root deeper.

Many Onion growers, who make a specialty of the business, find it is economical to alternate the crop with a green crop, such as German Millet, which can be cut for hay in July, and the "stubble" plowed down in August, giving a fresh fibrous soil, *clear of weeds*, for the Onion crop to be sown next spring. It is not claimed that the alternation of a green crop with the Onions is a necessity, as it is well known that the Onion is one of the very few crops that does not seem benefited by alternating; but it is claimed that it gives almost entire freedom from weeds, as after a crop of Millet which has been cut before its seed ripens, few troublesome weeds will come up the next year.

MANURES.

I have always held the opinion, that when well-rotted stable manure, whether from horses or cows, can be procured, at a cost not exceeding $3.00 per ton delivered on the ground, it is cheaper and better than any kind of concentrated fertilizer. It should be plowed in at the rate of thirty tons per acre. The concentrated fertilizers in the market are now so numerous that it would be invidious to specify particular brands. We ourselves, except in using occasionally the "Blood and Bone Fertilizer," which we have proved to be excellent, use only pure ground bone and Peruvian guano, which, for Onions, we prefer to mix together in equal parts, sowing it on the land after plowing, at the rate of at least one ton per acre of the mixture, (when no stable manure has been used,) and after sowing to be harrowed in, as described in "Preparing the Ground."

One of the most valuable manures for the Onion crop are the droppings from the chicken or pigeon house, which, when mixed with twice their weight of lime, or coal or wood ashes, so as to disintegrate and pulverize them, may be sown on the land after plowing, to be harrowed in, at the rate of three or four tons per acre of the mixture. Night soil, when mixed with dry muck, coal ashes, charcoal dust, lime, or lime rubbish, as absorbents, and spread on after plowing at the rate of six or eight tons per acre, and harrowed deeply in, will never fail to produce a heavy crop of Onions in any suitable soil.

There are many other manures that will answer the purpose, often to be had in special localities, such as the refuse hops and "grains" from breweries, which should be used in the same manner and quantities as stable manure; while fish guano, whalebone shavings, or shavings from horn, when pulverized so as to be in proper condition to be taken up by the plants, are nearly equal in value to ground bone. Wood ashes alone, spread on at the rate of five or six tons per acre, will usually give excellent results.

It is well ever to keep the fact in mind, that it will always be more profitable to fertilize one acre of Onions well than two imperfectly. If thirty tons of stable manure or one and one-half tons of concentrated fertilizer are used to an acre, the net profits are almost certain to be larger than if that quantity had been spread over two acres; for in all probability nearly as much weight of crop would be got from the one well-manured acre as from the two that had been done imperfectly, besides the saving of seed and labor in cultivating two acres instead of one.

Preparing the Ground.

In preparing the ground for the reception of the seed, (if it has not been plowed the fall previous,) plowing should be begun as soon as the land is dry enough to work, first having spread over the land well-rotted stable manure, at the rate of thirty tons to the acre. This should be lightly turned under, plowing not more than five or six inches deep, and covering the manure so that it will be three or four inches under the surface. For this reason, the manure must be well rotted, otherwise it cannot be well covered by the plow. If concentrated fertilizers are to be used, it is best to plow the land up roughly, sow the fertilizer at the rate of one to two tons per acre, according to its fertilizing properties, and then harrow thoroughly, so that it is regularly incorporated with the soil. After harrowing with an ordinary toothed harrow, the surface should be further leveled with some kind of a "smoothing" harrow, either Meeker's Smoothing Disc Harrow, or some sort of chain harrow. The former I like best, as the revolving discs pulverize the soil to a depth of three inches much better than it can be done by raking, and the smoothing board, which follows in the wake of the revolving wheels, makes the surface, if free from stones, smooth as a board, and far better than it can be done by raking.

Sowing the Seed.

The ground being thus prepared, the next thing is the sowing of the seed, about six pounds being used per acre. This, of course, now-a-days, is done always by the seed drilling machine, of which there are a dozen or more in the market, nearly all of which do the work well. In our business at the present date, we sell the Matthews and the Planet, Jr., giving the preference in the order in which they are named. In sowing the first row, a line must be stretched so as to have that line straight, after which the sower can readily regulate the other lines. The favorite distance for Onion rows to be placed apart is fifteen inches, though they are sometimes sown as close as twelve inches, leaving out every ninth row for an alley, thus forming them into beds of eight rows each. Where there is reason to believe weeds may be troublesome, this plan of forming in beds has the advantage of the alley (twenty-four inches wide) to throw the weeds in. I so firmly believe in the value of firming in the seeds after sowing, that I advise, in addition to the closing and firming of the seeds by the drill, to use a roller besides, particularly if the land is light, or where the soil has not been sufficiently firmed down.

Cultivating.

There is no crop where the adage of "a stitch in time" is so applicable as in the Onion crop; so that just as soon as the lines can be well seen, which will be in twenty or thirty days after sowing, apply the hand cultivator between the rows. There are a great many styles of hand cultivators. On light soils, the best we have used is known as the "Universal." The distance at which Onions should stand is from one to two inches, and if the crop is sown evenly and thinly few will require to be taken out; but whether it be weeds or Onions that are to be removed, one thing should never be lost sight of, that when this operation is done, every inch of the surface should be broken. This is best done after having been run through by the hand cultivator, by using a wooden lawn rake all over the land, lightly raking *across* the rows. It is one of the most common mistakes in a laborer when weeding or hoeing, if he sees no weeds, to pass over such portions without breaking the crust. By this neglect, he not only most likely passes another crop of weeds in embryo under the unbroken crust, but the portion unbroken loses the stirring so necessary for the well-being of the crop. In my long experience in garden operations, I have had more trouble to keep the workmen up to the mark in this matter than in any other; and I never fail, when I discover a man in such negligence, to set him back over his work until he does it properly; and if he again fails to do so, promptly dismiss him.

HARVESTING.

The Onion crop is usually fit to harvest in this section from the 5th to the 20th of August; that is, when the seed has been sown in early spring, which should be not later than May 1st, if possible, and if by April 1st, all the better. If the seed be sown too late, it may delay the time of ripening, which may result in a complete loss of the crop; for if the bulbs are not ripened by August, there is danger, if September is wet, that they will not ripen at all; hence the great necessity of early seeding in spring. If the Onion crop is growing very strong, it will facilitate the ripening process by bending the leaves down with the back of a wooden rake, or some such implement, so as to "knee " them, as it is called, at the neck of the bulb. This checks the flow of sap and tends to ripen the bulb.

After the tops of the Onions become yellow and wither up, they should be pulled without unnecessary delay; for if continued wet weather should occur and delay the pulling too long, a secondary growth of the roots may be developed, which would injure the crop seriously. After pulling, lay the bulbs in convenient rows, so as to cover the ground, but not to lay on each other. By turning them every day or two, in six or eight days they will usually be dry enough to be carted to their storage quarters, where the shriveled tops are cut off, and the Onions stored on slatted shelves, to the depth of six or eight inches, in some dry and airy place.

It is of importance to have the bottom of the shelves slatted, so as to leave spaces an inch or so apart, that air may be admitted at the bottom as well as the top of the heap. The shelves, when all the space at hand is to be made available, may be constructed one above another. But if to be kept through the winter, they must be protected in some building capable of resisting severe frost, or covered with hay or straw, as a protection against extreme cold; for although the Onion will stand a moderate degree of frost, yet any long continuation of a zero temperature would injure it. When frozen they should never be handled, as in that condition they are easily blemished and would rot. When kept in barrels, holes should be bored in the sides, and they should be left unheaded until shipped, so as to permit the escape of any moisture that may be generated.

INSECTS AND OTHER ENEMIES.

For such insects as attack the Onion crop, I am much afraid there are few, if any, effective remedies. Every year's experience with the enemies that attack plants in the open field convinces me that with very few of them can we successfully cope. The remedy, if remedy it is, for rust, smut, or other mildew parasites, must, in my opinion, be a preventive one; that is, whenever practicable, use new land or renew the old land by a green crop, such as Rye, Timothy, or Millet, in all sections subject to these diseases. The same plan had better be adopted in all sections where the Onion maggot, or other insects, attacks the crop.

The theory for this practice is, that it is believed that nearly all plants affected by insects or disease have such *peculiar to themselves*, and that the germs lie in the soil ready to fasten on the *same* crop, if planted without intermission on the same ground, while if a season intervenes the larva or germ has nothing congenial to feed on, and is, in consequence, destroyed. In practice, we usually find that cultivated land "rested" for a season by a grass crop gives always a cleaner and healthier crop to whatever vegetable follows it. In cases, however, where the land cannot be rested, or when it has been rested to be cropped in spring, it is a great preventive of the ravages of all kinds of insects to plow the land in the fall as late as possible, so as to disturb the larvæ of insects and expose them to the action of frosts and rains.

THE PRODUCT.

The average product of the Onion crop varies very much, ranging from 300 to 900 bushels per acre, the mean being about 600 bushels per acre. The price is variable like all perishable commodities, ranging from fifty cents per bushel, the price at which they usually wholesale in the New York market in fall, to $1 or $1.50 per bushel for winter and spring prices. The estimate, then, of profit per acre may be given about as follows:

Manure, per acre........................ $72 00
Plowing, weeding, and harvesting crop, per
   acre................................... 100 00
6 lbs. seed, average $2 per lb............. 12 00
Rent or interest on land, per acre......... 9 00
Marketing crop, per acre................. 7 00

$200 00

600 bushels per acre, at 50c.............. $300 00
Cost..................................... 200 00

Profit................................... $100 00

This estimate is a moderate one; for if the crop is sold in spring, the chances are that the profit may be two or three times as much.

Onions Sold Green.

All the foregoing relates to the Onion crop ripened; but in all large cities immense quantities of Onions are sold in the green state, many of them before they have attained half their growth. To get the earliest crop of Onions in this condition, the Onion sets are used, which are small Onions from the size of a pea to the size of three-quarters of an inch in diameter; but the smaller the better, as they make a crop nearly as quick and never run to seed, while the larger ones occasionally do. Onion sets must all be planted by hand, in rows made by the garden marker at about nine inches apart, and the sets being planted from two to three inches apart. They are most conveniently planted in beds of eight rows each, leaving a space of eighteen inches for an alley-way.

The green Onions are tied in bunches of eight or ten

each, and often sell at eight and ten cents per bunch. The crop is usually begun to be marketed by the middle of June, and is sold off by the middle of July. This garden crop of Onions is usually heavier manured and requires more labor than the field crop, but its market value is often three times that of the field crop. Onions are also sown in this way when grown from seed, but of course this matures two or three weeks later, and is not usually so remunerative as the green crop from the sets.

Potato Onions.

These are increased by the bulb, as it grows, splitting into six, eight, or ten sections, which form the crop from which the "set" or root for next season's planting is obtained. The sets are planted in early spring, in rows one foot apart, the Onions three or four inches between, and, like the Onions raised from sets, are generally sold green, as in that state they are very tender, while in the dry state they are less desirable than the ordinary Onion.

Top Onions.

Top Onions, so called, are propagated by the peculiar property of this variety of Onion producing a cluster of small bulblets on the Onion stalk. An excrescence of bulblets is formed instead of flowers and seeds. In all respects its culture is the same as the Potato Onion, only that, as the bulbs are smaller, they can be planted closer.

Shallots.

A vegetable nearly allied to the Potato Onion, only that it never forms an individual bulb but always grows in clusters. It is planted in the fall, the same distance apart as the Potato Onion, and starts to grow on the first opening of spring, so that the crop is usually marketed in May.

Varieties of the Onion.

We here give a short description and illustrations of the leading varieties of Onions. The seeds of Onions have heretofore been raised mainly in Connecticut, Massachusetts, Rhode Island, and Michigan, but of late years large quantities have been raised in California. A prejudice against that raised in California originated in consequence of the first lots raised there being from inferior stocks, but later experience has shown us beyond question that, when the quality of the stock from which the seed was raised has been the same as used in the Eastern States, the crop has been in all respects equal. In our "trial grounds," where upward of fifty stocks of Onions are tested annually, we find that the California raised seed is in no way inferior to that raised in Connecticut or Massachusetts.

Onion seed loses its germinating power sooner than almost any other seed, and, unless the sample is very fine indeed, it is of little use the second year. This is the reason for the great disparity in the price of seeds, for as the Onion seed crop is a very uncertain one, and from its germinating qualities being limited so that no stock can be held over, the price in different seasons fluctuates from $1 to $5 per pound.

134 GARDEN AND FARM TOPICS.

EXTRA EARLY RED ONION.

FIRST EARLY, EXTRA EARLY FLAT RED. A thin, rather light colored Onion, and a good keeper, but earliest of all.

LARGE RED WETHERSFIELD. One of the favorite sorts for the general crop, and a good keeper and yielder.

YELLOW GLOBE DANVERS. A half-globe shaped stock, one of the best yielders and a splendid keeper.

EARLY RED GLOBE. One of the earliest of the Globe varieties, smaller than the *Large* Red Globe.

LARGE RED GLOBE. Later and larger than the last, but a favorite market sort, and a perfect globe shape.

SOUTHPORT LARGE WHITE GLOBE. One of the best, and a favorite sort in New York markets, always bringing the highest price.

SOUTHPORT LARGE YELLOW GLOBE. Similar to the White

LARGE RED WETHERSFIELD ONION.

Globe, except in color, and a good keeper.

WHITE PORTUGAL, OR SILVER SKIN. One of the leading sorts of white flat Onion, a most excellent keeper and good yielder.

YELLOW DUTCH. A flat yellow Onion, a good yielder, but not so desirable as the other yellow sorts, on account of its color and shape. This and the *Flat* Yellow Danvers are very similar. One of the heaviest croppers.

YELLOW GLOBE DANVERS ONION.

Italian varieties well adapted for growing in the Southern States:

QUEEN. The earliest of all Onions, small, flat, white, and mild flavored.

NEAPOLITAN MARZAJOLE. An early white flat Onion, fine flavor.

LARGE WHITE ITALIAN TRIPOLI. Grows to a large size, and is later

SOUTHPORT LARGE YELLOW GLOBE ONION.

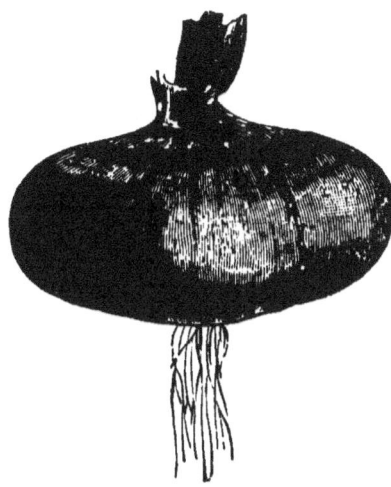

WHITE PORTUGAL, OR SILVER SKIN ONION.

than either of the preceding.

LARGE RED ITALIAN TRIPOLI. Similar to the preceding, except in color.

GIANT ROCCA. A very large-growing globe-shaped variety of a reddish brown color; flavor mild and sweet.

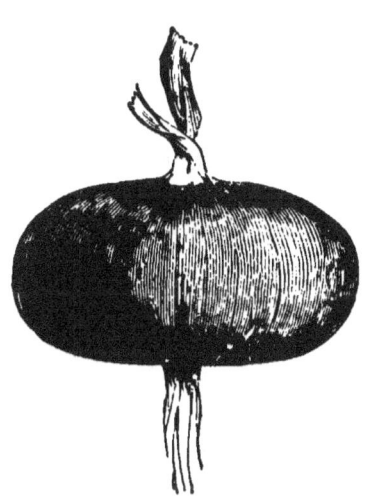

YELLOW DUTCH ONION.

HOW TO GROW CABBAGE AND CAULIFLOWER,

(EARLY AND LATE.)

IN answer to hundreds of inquiries that are made to me each season in relation to the various phases of Cabbage and Cauliflower culture, I find it necessary to write a special article on this subject, much of the information given being in reply to and in anticipation of the various questions that have been and are likely to be asked.

SOIL.

Cabbage is much easier managed than Cauliflower, and is, consequently, more certain of giving a crop, even under unfavorable conditions. The first condition of success with the Cabbage crop, like that of nearly every other vegetable, is the right kind of *soil*. The best soil for Cabbage is a rather sandy loam, not less than ten inches deep, the subsoil under which should be sand or gravel; a clayey or stiff subsoil is uncongenial to almost every crop. Not only does it delay operations in spring, as such soils dry slowly, but even when fit to work, the labor on soils having a clay or "hard pan" subsoil is nearly twice that of lighter soils, and usually with less satisfactory results. It may be superfluous to say that, unless the soil for Cabbage is drained artificially or naturally, (by a sand or gravel subsoil,) success is impossible. This, of course, is true of nearly every crop grown.

The proper pulverizing of the soil is a matter of the utmost importance. Although many of the large market gardens in Europe are yet dug with the spade or digging fork, it is rare that anything else is used with us than the plow and harrow. We ourselves are so satisfied of the superiority of the plow, as a pulverizer of the soil, over the spade or digging fork, that we would not allow our grounds, for any purpose, to be dug, even if done for nothing, and no digging is ever done on our grounds in any spot where horses can be worked. Experience has shown us that it is always beneficial to plow land in the fall, not only that when thus thrown up in ridges it gets pulverized by the action of the frost, but also that the turning up of the soil exposes the larvæ and eggs of insects also to the frost, which tends greatly to lessen their numbers the succeeding year.

Manure Heap.

When the ground to be used for the crop is far off from the manure yard, it is advantageous to have the manure placed in convenient heaps on the land, say of 100 or 200 loads in each, but care should be taken that the heap is not spread over too large a surface, as, (if the land has been heavily manured the previous year,) wherever the manure heap has lain, it will so "poison" the land that nothing will grow. If, however, the land is newly broken, never having been manured, where the manure has lain the crop will likely be the best. A good height for the manure heap is from four to six feet. For the early Cabbage crop, it should always be spread on broadcast, and in quantity not less than 100 cart loads, or 75 tons to the acre, which will leave it, when spread, about two or three inches in thickness.

HOW TO GROW CABBAGE AND CAULIFLOWER.

It is not usual that much choice can be made in stable manure, but when such is the case, equal portions of cow and horse manure are preferable; not that there is much difference in value, weight for weight, but that it is advantageous to have the manure of the cow stable mixed with that of the horse, so as to prevent the violent heating of the horse manure, which, if not repeatedly turned, will generate heat so as to cause it to "fire-fang" or burn, which renders it comparatively useless. Always bear in mind that the more thoroughly rotted and disintegrated manure can be had, the better will be the results. When manure is thoroughly rotted and short, it may be turned in by the plow just as it is spread on the land; but if long, it is necessary to draw it into the furrow ahead of the plow, so that it is completely covered in.

After plowing in the manure, and before the ground is harrowed, our best growers in the vicinity of New York sow from 400 to 500 pounds of guano or bone dust, and then harrow it deeply in, and smooth over with the back of the harrow, when the bed is ready to receive the plants.

VARIETIES TO PLANT.

In the vicinity of New York, and, in fact, now wherever the business of market gardening is intelligently followed, the best varieties of Cabbage for the *early* crop are recognized to be the "Early Jersey Wakefield" and "Henderson's Early Summer" for general culture, and to describe others of the scores named would be only confusing. The "Jersey Wakefield" is the earlier, and is a little smaller. Our prize head received in June, 1883, from Mr. J. B. Souders, Vinton, Iowa, weighed 17 pounds. It is planted usually 28 inches between the rows and 16 inches between the plants, thus requiring from 10,000 to 12,000 plants per acre. The "Early Summer" grows a little larger. Our prize head, received in August, 1883, weighed 24 pounds. It was grown by

HENDERSON'S SELECTED EARLY JERSEY WAKEFIELD CABBAGE.

Mr. George Hattie, Fallston, Penn. It should be planted 30 inches apart and 18 inches between the plants, requiring from 8,000 to 10,000 per acre.

The reason for placing the rows so wide apart and the plants so close in the rows is to admit of a row of Lettuce, Spinach, or Radishes between the rows of Cabbage. All of these vegetables mature quickly, and can be cut out before the Cabbage grows enough to interfere with them, and it is necessary that this double crop should be taken off the land so as to help pay for the manure that is so lavishly used, but which is absolutely necessary to produce a good crop of Cabbages. Where early Cabbage is grown alone, it would be better to plant about two or two and a half feet each way, so that cross cultivation can be done; and also, in cases where manure in sufficient quantities is not attainable, they are better thus planted when manure has to be applied in the hill. If applied in the hill, a good shovelful of stable manure

HENDERSON'S EARLY SUMMER CABBAGE.

should be used to each, mixing it well with the soil, but raising the "hill," so-called, no higher than the general surface.

RAISING OF CABBAGE PLANTS.

The raising of plants for the early crop is a very important point. The great majority of plants for the early crop are sown by the New York market gardeners between the 15th and 20th of September, that is, when the "Early Wakefield" is used; but the "Early Summer" should not be sown until the 25th to the 30th of September. Careful attention is given to have the sowings made as near as possible to these dates; for if earlier, *many of the plants will go to seed*, particularly the

"Early Summer" variety. Again, if much later than the dates last given, the season will be too far advanced, and the plants would not be strong enough to keep over winter in the cold frames.

A case occurred some years ago in Philadelphia, where a market gardener sowed "Early York" Cabbage on the 5th of September, and nearly every plant ran to seed. The gardener sued the seedsman for damages, and got non-suited, as he deserved, as the seedsman had no difficulty in showing that other gardeners who had purchased this same seed, and who had sown it at the proper time, (in that latitude 20th of September,) had no such bad results.

In about thirty days from the time Cabbage seed is sown in September, the plants are of the right size to "prick out," or transplant into the cold frames. The plant must be planted down to the first leaf, and the root well firmed with the dibber. About 500 plants are allowed for a 3×6 feet sash. The cold frame, as most gardeners know, is simply two boards run parallel six feet apart, the back board being ten inches and the front one seven or eight inches high. We generally have all our Cabbage plants transplanted here from the seed-bed to the cold frames by the 1st of November, and it seldom happens that we have the weather cold enough to have the sashes put on before the end of November.

We are repeatedly asked the question,

What Degree of Frost Cabbage Plants Will Stand

in the frames before being covered with the sash. Much depends on the condition of the plants. It sometimes happens, after the transplanting is finished in October, (we usually *begin* the transplanting in the frames about the 15th,) that we have a continuation of comparatively warm weather, which induces a quick and soft growth in the plants, which, of course, renders them very susceptible of injury from frost. When in that condition, we have seen them injured when the thermometer only marked 27° above zero, or but 5° of frost; while if gradually hardened by being exposed to chilly nights, they would receive no injury even when the thermometer marks 10° or 12° above zero. This will be well understood when we remember that in midwinter, when covered with sash alone, they sustain a cold, often for days together, of 10° *below* zero; but then, of course, they have been gradually inured to it. In sections of the country where the thermometer falls to 15° or 20° below zero, it will be necessary to use straw mats or shutters over the glass. At all times, from the time of putting sashes on in fall until taking them off in spring, (which is usually from the 15th of March to April 1st,) abundant ventilation should be given, so as to render them as hardy as possible. The sure indication that they are in the "frost proof" condition is when the leaves show a bluish color, which they get when they have been gradually hardened off.

Spring Sowing.

Although the most of the Jersey market gardeners still use the cold frames for growing the bulk of their early Cabbage crop, yet of late years the system of spring sowing and transplanting, and sometimes even without transplanting, is also used to a considerable extent. This is usually done by sowing the seeds thickly (about one ounce to three sashes) in a hot-bed or green-house about February 1st, and transplanting into a slight hot-bed about March 1st, placing about 600 or 700 in a 3×6 feet sash. The hot-beds must, of course, be carefully protected by straw mats from frost, and with the proper attention to ventilation and watering, fine plants can be obtained by April 1st. We ourselves have grown nearly a quarter of a million plants each spring in this manner for years with most satisfactory results.

COLD FRAMES.

Another plan is to sow the Cabbage seed in *cold* frames from the 15th of February to March 1st, or even later for second early. By this method one ounce of seed is enough for five or six sashes, and it had better be sown in rows at six inches apart, as thus sown the air gets better around the plants, making them stronger. When the seed is sown in the cold frames in this way, it is absolutely necessary that the frost should be excluded by covering the glass with straw mats and shutters; for, of course, unless kept above the point of freezing, the plants cannot grow. The cold frames to be used for this purpose should be placed in the warmest and most sheltered place possible; the soil should be light and well enriched with *short* manure, nicely dug, and leveled and raked for the reception of the seed. If sown in drills, they should be about two inches deep; if sown broadcast, it is best to "chip" the ground all over with a steel rake so as to sink the seed to the depth of an inch or so; but in both cases do not omit to firm the soil by patting the surface over with the back of the spade.

All these directions for spring-sown plants are given for the latitude of New York, where the operations of planting Cabbage plants in the open ground are usually begun about the 25th of March and finished by the middle of

April. For it must be always borne in mind that Cabbage, being a hardy plant, when wanted for an early crop, should be set out in spring in any section as soon as the land is dry enough to work. As a guide, we may say, that whenever spring crops of Rye, Wheat, or Oats can be sown, Cabbage may safely be planted in the open field; for if the plants have been properly hardened, they will not be injured after being planted out, even by eight or ten degrees of frost.

The conditions in the different Southern States are so varied that it is not easy to give directions. It may be taken, however, as a general rule, that in any section of the country where the thermometer does not fall *lower* than 15° *above* zero, Cabbage seed should be sown about October 1st, the plants left (without covering) in the seed-beds all winter, and transplanted to the open ground as soon as it is fit to work in the spring, say in February or March. In some sections, where the fall weather continues fine into November, transplanting is done in that month where the crop is to mature.

CULTIVATION.

After planting in the field, no crop takes so kindly to hoeing or cultivating as Cabbage. In ten days after the planting is finished, cultivation should begin. If the Cabbages have been set two or two and a half feet apart each way, then the horse cultivator is the best pulverizer; but if a crop has been sown or planted between the rows of Cabbage, then a hand or wheel hoe can only be used. We ourselves now use the wheel hoe exclusively, and find it a saving of three-fourths in labor, with the work better done.

The price at which early Cabbage is sold now varies so

much at different dates, and in different parts of the country, that it is impossible to give anything like accurate figures, the range being all the way from $2.00 to $12.00 per 100. Perhaps $4.00 would be a fair average for "Wakefield" and $5.00 for "Early Summer," so that, counting 11,0co as the average per acre of the former and 9,000 of the latter, we have respectively $440.00 per acre for "Wakefield" and $450.00 for "Early Summer." These are the wholesale prices for large markets like New York. In smaller cities, where the product is sold direct to the consumer, one-third more would likely be obtained.

LATE CABBAGE.

These are such as mature during the months of September, October, and November, the seed for which is sown in open ground in May or June. Perhaps the best date for sowing for the general crop is about the 1st of June. We always prefer to sow Cabbage seed for this purpose in rows, ten or twelve inches apart, treading in the seed with the feet after sowing and before covering. We then level with a rake lengthwise with the rows, and roll or beat down with the back of a spade, so as to exclude the air from the soil and from the seed. Sown in this way, Cabbage seed will come up strongly in the driest weather, and is less likely to be afflicted with the black flea than if it made a feeble growth.

As the ground used for late Cabbage only yields one crop, it will not often pay, unless manure is cheap and abundant, to use it in the profusion required for the early Cabbage, so that it is usual to manure in the hill, as is done for the early crop, with stable manure; but when that is not attainable, some concentrated fertilizer, such as bone dust or guano, should be used, applying a good handful to each hill, but being careful, of course, to mix it well with the soil for about nine or ten inches deep and wide. In this way about 300 pounds per acre will be needed, when 6,000 or 7,000 plants are set on an acre. In our practice, we find nothing better than pure bone dust and guano mixed together. For further information on this subject, see *Essay on Manures and Modes of Application.*

Transplanting Cabbage.

In transplanting from the seed-bed to the open field in summer, the work is usually done in a dry and hot season, (the end of June or July;) and here, again, we give our oft-repeated warning of the absolute necessity of having every plant properly firmed. If the planting is well done with the dibber, it may be enough; but it is often not well done, and as a measure of safety it is always best to turn back on the rows after planting, and press alongside of each plant with the foot. This is quickly done, and it besides rests the planter, so that he can with greater vigor start on the next row.

In some sections of the country, particularly in the New England States, six or eight Cabbage seeds are put in the hills, and when the plants are of the height of two or three inches they are thinned out to one plant in each hill. This we think not only a slower method, but is otherwise objectionable, inasmuch as it compels us to place the manure in the ground for three or four weeks before the plant can take it up, to say nothing of the three or four weeks' culture necessary to be done before the seedlings in the hill get to the size of the plants when set out.

The cultivation of late Cabbage is in all respects similar

to that of early, except that it is usually planted alone. The work is done entirely by the horse cultivator, the rows and plants in the rows being, according to the kind, from twenty-four to thirty inches apart. There are a great number of kinds offered in the different seed lists, but experienced cultivators confine themselves to but very few kinds. These I give in the order in which they are most approved: "Henderson's Selected Flat Dutch," "American Drumhead," and "Marblehead Mammoth."

In addition to these, the "American Drumhead Savoy" is grown to a considerable extent, and it is really surprising that it is not grown to the exclusion of nearly all other sorts, as it attains nearly as much weight of crop, and is much more tender and finer in flavor. The "Green Scotch" and "Brown German Kale" belong to the Cabbage family, but do not form heads. The curled leaves of the whole plant can be used, and are, like the "Savoy," much finer in flavor than the plain head Cabbages, particularly after having been subjected to the frost in fall.

KEEPING CABBAGES IN WINTER.

There are various methods of doing this. It is best to leave them out as late as possible, so that they can be lifted before being frozen in. In this latitude, they can be safely left out until the third week in November. They are then dug or pulled up, according to the nature of the soil, and turned upside down (the roots up, the heads down) just where they have been growing, and the heads placed closely together in beds, six or eight feet wide, with alleys of about the same width between, care being taken to have the ground leveled, so that the Cabbages will set evenly together.

They can be left in this way for three or four weeks, or as long as the ground remains so that it can be dug in the alleys between the beds, the soil from which is thrown in on the beds of Cabbage, so that, when finished, they have a covering of six or seven inches of soil, or sufficient to cover the roots completely up. Sometimes they are covered up immediately on being lifted, by plowing a furrow, shoveling it out wide enough to receive the heads, then plowing so as to cover up, and so on till beds six or eight feet wide are thus formed. This plan is the quickest, but it has the disadvantage, if the season proves mild, of having the Cabbages covered up too soon by the soil, and hence there is more danger of decay. After the ground is frozen, stable litter, straw, or leaves, to the depth of three or four inches, should be thrown over the Cabbage beds, so as to prevent excessive freezing, and to facilitate the getting at the Cabbages in hard weather.

INSECTS.

The insects that attack the Cabbage tribe are various, and for some of them I regret to say that we are almost helpless in arresting their ravages. Young Cabbage plants in fall, or in hot-beds in spring, are often troubled with the *Aphis*, or, as it is popularly known, the "Green Fly" or "Green Louse." This is easily destroyed by having the plants dusted over once or twice with tobacco dust. This same insect, of a blue color, is often disastrous to the growing crop in the field; and on its first appearance, tobacco dust should be applied, as, of course, if the Cabbages are headed up, it could not be used.

Another insect which attacks them in these stages is a species of slug or small caterpillar; a green, glutinous insect, about one-fourth or one-half of an inch in length.

This is not quite so easily destroyed as the other, but will succumb to a mixture of one part white hellebore to four parts lime dust, sprinkled on thick enough to slightly whiten the plants. This same remedy I have found to be the most efficacious in preventing the ravages of the Black Flea, or "Jumping Jack," that is often so destructive to Cabbage plants sown or planted in the open ground during May and June; but in this case its application may have to be repeated daily, often for two weeks.

Another most troublesome insect is the Cabbage Caterpillar, which attacks the crop often when just beginning to head. This is the larva of a species of small yellow butterfly, which deposits its eggs on the crop in May or June. When fields of Cabbage are isolated, or where neighbors can be found to act in unison, the best plan is to catch the butterflies with an insect-catching net as soon as they show themselves. This is the most effective and quickest way to get rid of them. However, if that has been neglected, the caterpillar can be destroyed by dusting white hellebore on the Cabbages; but, of course, this cannot be done when the heads are matured enough to be ready to use, as the hellebore is to some extent poisonous, though, used when the plants are about half grown, it will do no harm, as the rains will have washed it sufficiently off by the time they head up.

A correspondent from Michigan recommends a solution of common alum, made by dissolving one pound of alum in three gallons of water. This, he says, will effectually destroy the Cabbage Worm on Cabbage. I have not yet had an opportunity to test it, but it seems a rational remedy, and has the advantage of being cheap and of not being poisonous to human beings. The solution is best made by dissolving the alum in boiling water, and then adding cold water to make it of the requisite strength.

HOW TO GROW CABBAGE AND CAULIFLOWER. 151

It should be sprinkled over the Cabbage or Cauliflower plants every two or three days until the worms have disappeared. It is also recommended for all plants that are affected by worms or caterpillars.

The insects here described are not, probably, all that afflict the Cabbage crop. A letter just received from a gentleman in Montgomery, Alabama, says that the young Cabbage plants in that region are often swept off in twenty-four hours by a small green worm; a species of slug or caterpillar, no doubt. The remedy for all such is white hellebore powder, which had better be dusted on the plants once a week as a *preventive*, before the insect makes its appearance. In fact, all remedies against insects are best used as preventives, or, at least, on the very first appearance of the pests.

But the insect enemies that attack the *roots* of the Cabbage are not so easy to destroy. In fact, with the Wire Worm and Cabbage Maggot we are almost helpless, so far as my experience has gone. For the latter, which is the worst enemy, a remedy has recently been recommended to me, which, as yet, I have had no opportunity to test. It is to make a hole with the dibber, five or six inches deep, close to the root of each plant, and drop into it nine or ten drops of bi-sulphide of carbon, and closing up the hole again. An observing market gardener from central New York has saved his Cabbage and Cauliflower plants from the maggots for years by observing that the eggs are laid close to the stem of the Cabbage. When half grown, the maggots are no larger than a pin's head, and are loosely attached to the stems of the Cabbage. One movement of the finger displaces them, and no further harm ensues. The eggs are deposited by a fly about half the size of the common house fly, usually here about the middle of May, when the Cabbage starts to grow. Last year the Cabbage and Cauliflower in our "trial grounds" were attacked by the Cabbage Maggot at the roots early in May. A small handful of Peruvian guano was at once strewn around each plant and hoed in around the roots. This at once started an unusual vigor of growth, which sustained the plants until they matured excellent heads. Understand, the guano probably did not injure the insect; it only enabled the Cabbage to outgrow its attack.

CLUB ROOT.

For the destruction of the insect which causes the excrescence known as "club root" in Cabbage, a heavy dressing of lime in fall and spring will check it to a great extent. In fact, on lands adjacent to the shores of New York Bay, where the soil is mixed with oyster shell, "club root" is rarely seen, Cabbage having been grown on some fields successively for fifty years without a trace of it being seen, showing that the insect that causes the "club root" cannot exist in contact with lime; for it is found that on lands where there is no oyster shell deposit, a quarter of a mile distant, Cabbages cannot be grown two years in succession on the same land, unless heavily dressed with lime, and even then it is always deemed safest never to plant Cabbages two years in succession on the same ground; for while such crops as Onions show but little benefit by rotation with other crops, Cabbages, perhaps more than anything else, are benefited by such alternation. When it can be done, nothing is better than to let the Cabbage crop be alternated with grasses, such as German Millet, Timothy, or Clover, or a crop of Oats or Rye. This is the method pursued by many of the Long Island market gardeners, who grow for the New York market, where their lands are cheap enough to allow them to do so; but the gardeners of Hudson County, New Jersey, which is in sight of New York city, whose lands now are limited in area, and for which an average of $50.00 per acre rent is paid per annum, cannot well afford to let their lands lay thus comparatively idle, and in consequence do not now raise as fine crops as the lands thus "rested" by the grass or grain crops.

If the land for the Cabbage crop is of a kind suitable to grow a good crop of Corn or Potatoes, and is tilled or fertilized in the manner advised, it is rare indeed that a crop will fail to head, if the plants are in good condition, and have been properly planted, unless they are attacked by the maggot or "club root." In our trial grounds, where over a hundred different stocks of Cabbage are tested each year, we have found that every kind of Cabbage tested, early or late, has produced solid heads, showing *that when the conditions are right all kinds of Cabbages will head up and produce a crop.*

A circumstance came under our notice in the summer of 1882, which well illustrates the necessity for care in planting. We had sold, some time in February, a large lot of our "Early Summer" Cabbage seed to two market gardeners in Rochester, N. Y. The orders were filled from the same bag of seed. Some time about the end of June one of the men wrote, saying that he had evidently got some spurious kind of Cabbage from us, as his neighbor was marketing his crop, while in his field of ten acres he had not a head fit to cut, nor were there any appearance of their ever doing so, he thought. Investigation showed that no maggot, "club root," or other insect was affecting the roots; the land was nearly identical with that which had made a successful crop, and had been equally well manured and cultivated. So the only *probable* solution of the matter was, that the plants in the case of failure had been *loosely planted*, and had failed to make a prompt start, as in the other case where the planting had been properly done, so that, while the one lot advanced without a check, the growth of the other lot was arrested. This was most likely to have been the case, for there could be no cause for the difference unless on some such hypothesis.

But there was a fortunate sequel to the case. It luckily happened that a heavy rain storm occurred while the Cabbages were yet in this unheaded condition. This started, as it were, a second growth, which resulted in their forming splendid heads by August 1st, at a time when Cabbages were scarce, which, luckily for the owner, brought a much higher price than they would had they matured at the proper season, in June or July. In fact, the head that obtained our $20 prize for the best "Early Summer Cabbage in 1882 was cut from this lot, and weighed twenty pounds. The result was fortunate for us, who had sold the seed; for, had not rain come so opportunely, the crop might never have headed up, and it would then have been hard to convince the man that he had not been furnished with spurious seed.

CAULIFLOWER.

WHAT has been advised for Cabbage crops, either early or late, is exactly the culture necessary for a crop of Cauliflower, except that Cauliflower, being a plant of more delicate constitution, requires to be more carefully handled. For instance, where the Cabbage plants in the cold frames will keep safely over winter in this latitude, with no covering but the glass sash, Cauliflower plants

HENDERSON'S EARLY SNOWBALL CAULIFLOWER.

require the use of straw mats over the sashes, as the plant is much more easily hurt by frost. In fact, it is better never to keep the plants through the winter; those sown in February, and transplanted into cold frames in March, and planted in the open ground in April, as recommended for spring-sown Early Cabbage, being better. The plants, however, must be started early enough, so that they can be set out not later than the middle of April; for if not rooted well before warm weather sets in, they will either "button," (that is, form small, stunted flowers,) or else fail entirely to head up.

Cauliflower delights in a cool atmosphere, and never does well when the season is hot and dry, unless complete irrigation can be given when the plant is about half grown. If this can be done the crop is certain. We ourselves grew in this manner nearly an acre for many years, the crop selling for an average of $1,200 per acre annually, and that was before we had introduced the now famous variety known as "*Henderson's Early Snowball*," which is ahead of all other kinds in its certainty to make a crop. The next in succession to this is the "Early Erfurt," which is again succeeded by the "Early Paris," but neither of these in any respect is equal to the "Snowball." For late crop the varieties known as "Algiers" and "Erfurt" are the kinds usually grown. The plants are obtained by sowing at the same dates as for late Cabbages. It is planted three feet each way, and cultivated exactly as late Cabbages, and often sells as high as $25.00 per 100 in November and December. We are of the opinion, however, that the "Snowball," of which twice the number can be grown per acre, will prove a more profitable crop, even for late, than the "Algiers," as it is certainly more certain to form heads. It is not once in twenty years that a variety of vegetables or fruit makes such an advance in earliness and quality as this "Snowball" Cauliflower, and we have much satisfaction in the knowledge that we were the first to bring it into cultivation, about five years ago. It is now grown to almost the entire exclusion of all other early kinds of Cauliflower in this country, and hundreds have succeeded, both North and South, in raising a crop from this variety, who had previously completely failed with all other kinds.

In Cauliflowers, as in Cabbages, it is folly to attempt the experiment of many kinds. Long experience has taught us that two or three of each, for early and second early, are all sufficient. Although our seed catalogues enumerate scores of kinds, gardeners, who know what they are about, fight shy of all except those whose merit has been proved beyond any question of a doubt. For this reason, we only give the names of such as we *know* to be the *best*.

There are few vegetables that we cultivate that are so eccentric in their modes of development as the Cauliflower, and many market gardeners have, to their sorrow, lost entire crops by experimenting here with untried kinds. One of our best New Jersey market gardeners being over in England a few years ago, procured seed of a variety of Cauliflower that was exclusively used as the best for the London market. To be safe he got stock of it from three different market gardeners, the seed being raised from the stock they were then marketing. He sowed the seed, and planted out about an equal number of plants of each, together with a lot of Snowball. All were sown and planted exactly alike. The "London Market" grew nearly three feet high, but did not form one head in twenty, and these were late, while from the "Snowball" lot nearly every head was marketable, maturing ten days earlier. In all probability, however, in the cooler climate of England the "London Market" would have proved better than the "Snowball."

ON THE GROWING AND PRESERVING

OF

CELERY FOR WINTER.

THE seeds are sown on a well-pulverized, rich border, in the open ground, as early in the season as the ground can be worked. (For instructions in sowing. see article headed " *Use of the Feet in Sowing and Planting.*") The bed is kept clear of weeds until July, when the plants are set out for the crop. But as the seedling plants are rather troublesome to raise, when for private use only, and as they can usually be purchased cheaper than they can be raised on a small scale, it is scarcely worth while to sow the seed. But when wanted in quantity, the plants should always be raised by the grower, as Celery plants are not only difficult to transplant, but are usually too expensive to buy when the crop is grown to sell.

PLANTING ON THE SURFACE.

The European plan is to make a trench six or eight inches deep in which to plant the Celery; but our violent rain storms in summer soon showed us that this plan was not a good one here, so we set about planting on the level surface of the ground, just as we do with all vegetables.

Celery requires an abundance of manure, which, as usual with all other crops, must be well mixed and incorporated with the soil before the Celery is set out. When the ground is well prepared, we stretch a line to the distance required, walk on it, or beat it slightly with a spade, so that it leaves a mark to show where to place the plants. These are set out at distances of six inches between the plants, and usually four feet between the rows, when the Celery is to be "banked" up for early or fall use; but when grown for winter use, from two to three feet between the rows are sufficient. Great care must be taken, in putting out the Celery, to see that the plant is set just to the depth of the roots; if much deeper, the "heart" might be too much covered up, which would impede the growth. It is also important that the soil be well packed to the roots in planting, and this we do by returning on each row, after planting, and pressing the soil against each plant firmly with the feet; and if the operation can be done in the evening, and the plants copiously watered, no further attention will be required, particularly if the soil has been freshly dug or plowed.

Handling and Banking Up.

Planting may be done at any time from the 25th of July to the first week in August. After planting, nothing is to be done but keep the crop clear of weeds until September. By that time the handling process is to be begun, which consists in drawing the earth to each side of the Celery, and pressing it tightly to it, so as to give the leaves an upward growth preparatory to blanching for use.

Supposing this handling process is done by the middle of September, by the first week in October it is ready for "banking up," which is done by digging the soil from between the rows, and laying or banking it up with the spade on each side of the row of Celery. After being so banked up in October, it will be ready for use in three or four weeks, if wanted at that time. But if, as in most cases, it is needed for winter use only, and is to be put away in trenches, or in the cellar, as will hereafter be described, all that it requires is the operation of "handling." If the Celery is to be left in the open ground where it was grown, then a heavy bank must be made on each side of the rows, and as cold weather approaches, (say in this latitude by the middle of November,) an additional covering of a least a foot of leaves or litter must be closely packed against the bank, to protect it from frost; but it is not safe to leave it in the banks where it grows, in any section of the country where the temperature gets lower than $10°$ above zero.

PRESERVING IN CELLARS.

Perhaps the best way to keep Celery for family use is in a cool cellar. This can be done by storing it in narrow boxes, of a depth a little less than the height of the Celery. A few inches of sand or soil are placed in the bottom of the box, and the Celery is packed upright, the roots being placed on the sand or soil at the bottom; *but no sand or soil must be put between the stalks of the Celery,* all that is needed being the damp sand on the bottom of the box; the meaning of which is, that before Celery will blanch or whiten, it must first start at the root; hence the necessity of placing the roots on an inch or so of damp sand.

Boxes thus packed and placed in a cool cellar in November will be blanched fit for use during January, February, and March; though for succession it will be better to put it in the boxes, from the open ground, at three different times, say October 25th, November 10th, and November 20th. If the boxes, however, are not at hand, the Celery may be put away on the floor of the cellar, in strips of eight or nine inches wide, divided by boards of a width equal to the height of the Celery. That is, if the Celery is two feet high, the boards separating it must be about the same height. The reason for dividing the Celery in these narrow strips by boards is to prevent heating, which would occur if placed together in too thick masses. The dates above given apply, of course, to the latitude of New York; if further south, do the work later; if further north, earlier.

PRESERVING IN TRENCHES.

If one has no suitable cellar, the Celery can be very readily preserved in the manner followed by market gardeners. Thus, after it has been "handled" or straightened up, as before described, what is intended for use by Christmas should be dug up about October 25th; that to be used in January and February, by November 10th; and that for March use, by November 20th, which latter date is as late as it can be risked here. Although it will stand quite a sharp frost, the weather by the end of November is often severe enough to kill it, or so freeze it in the ground that it cannot be dug up. The ground in which it is to be preserved for winter use must be as dry as possible, and so arranged that no water can remain in the trench. Dig a trench as narrow as possible, (it should not be wider than ten inches,) and of a depth equal to the height of the Celery; that is, if the plant of Celery be eighteen inches high, the trench should be dug eighteen inches deep. The Celery is then packed exactly in the manner described for storing in boxes to be placed in the cellar; that is, stand it as near upright as possible, and pack as closely together as can be done without bruising it. No soil or sand must be put between the stalks. As the weather becomes cold, the trenches should be gradually covered with leaves or litter to the thickness of six or eight inches, which will be enough to prevent severe freezing, and enable the roots to be taken out easily when wanted.

Another method now practised by the market gardeners of New Jersey is as follows : before the approach of very cold weather, (say the middle of December,) the Celery in the trenches is pressed somewhat closely together by passing a spade down deeply alongside of the trench on each side, but about three or four inches from the Celery. It is best done by two men, so that they press against each other, thus firming the top of the Celery in the trench until it is compact enough to sustain a weight of three or four inches of soil, which is taken from the sides of the trench and spread over the Celery. This earth covering keeps it rather fresher than the covering of litter, though, on the approach of cold weather, the earth covering is not sufficient, and a covering of six or seven inches of leaves must yet be placed over the earth covering.

Varieties to Grow.

From 200 to 500 roots are usually required for use by an ordinary family. The varieties I recommend are the Half Dwarf, Golden Dwarf, Sandringham, White Walnut, and London Red. The red is as yet but little used in this country, though the flavor is better, and the plant altogether hardier than the white. A new variety, known as the Parsley leaved, has just been introduced, which will be very useful for table decoration, as well as for all purposes for which Celery is used, as it is equally as good as any of the others.

RUST.

I am often asked for the cause of and remedy for Celery rusting or burning. The cause, I think, is the condition of the weather, which destroys the tender fibers, or what are called the working roots of the plant; for I find it is usually worse in seasons of extreme drought or moisture, particularly in warm weather. It is exceedingly necessary, however, to have the land thoroughly pulverized before planting, as I have reason to believe that this being imperfectly done often tends greatly to increase the tendency to rust.

I know of no remedy, nor do I believe there is any. I may say, however, that it is less liable to appear on new, fresh soils, that are free from acids or sourness, than on old soils that have been surfeited with manure, and have had no rest.

PITH.

Although, under ordinary conditions, if proper varieties of Celery are used, the crop should never be pithy or hollow, yet I have found that now and then even the most solid kinds of Celery have become more or less hollow when planted in soft, loose soils, such as reclaimed peat bogs, where the soil is mostly composed of leaf mould. In fact, on heavy or clayey soils the Celery, and all other vegetables, will be specifically heavier than on lighter soils.

THE NEW CELERY, "WHITE PLUME."

This season, (1884,) for the first time, is introduced a new kind of Celery, that we feel satisfied will so simplify its culture, that the most inexperienced can now grow Celery, blanched in the proper condition for the table, just as easily as a Cabbage or Lettuce. The peculiarity of the Celery known as " White Plume " is, that *naturally* its stalks and portions of its inner leaves are white, so that, by closing the stalks, either by tying them up with matting, or by simply drawing the soil up against the plant and pressing it together with the hands, and again drawing up the soil with the hoe or plow, so as to keep the soil that has been squeezed against the Celery in its place, the work of blanching is completed; while it is well-known that in all other kinds of Celery, in addition to this, the slow and troublesome process of "banking" with the spade is a necessity.

Another great merit of the "White Plume" Celery is, that it far exceeds any known vegetable as an ornament for the table, the inner leaves being disposed somewhat like an ostrich feather, so as to suggest the name we have given it of " White Plume."

It is well known that one-half the value of a Celery, particularly in our best hotels and restaurants, is held to be its fitness as a table ornament, and for this purpose this new variety is admirably fitted. In addition to this, its eating qualities are equal to the very best of the older sorts, being *crisp, solid*, and having that nutty flavor peculiar to the "Walnut" and some of the red sorts. Altogether, I cannot find words sufficient to describe its many merits as it deserves.

The great bugbear in the cultivation of Celery, by

THE NEW CELERY, "WHITE PLUME."

those engaged in growing it for market, has been the labor entailed in the "banking" to whiten or blanch it; and with the unskilled amateur growing a few hundred for private use, the troublesome process of "banking" has usually been a detriment sufficient to prevent him from trying. Now he can grow this new sort, as I have before stated, just as easily as Cabbage or Lettuce. In the first week of October of 1882, the Celery banks in Hudson County, New Jersey, must have cost at least $15,000 in labor to erect; but a rain storm of twenty-four hours' duration washed the banks down and destroyed the work of weeks. Had this new Celery been under process of blanching, no high banks would have been needed, and the storm would have been nearly harmless, as the "wash" would have done but a trifling injury.

But absolute perfection is hardly to be expected in anything, and the "White Plume" Celery has one drawback; the very qualities that make its culture so simple in the fall and early winter months, unfit it for a late Celery that will keep until spring, as its tenderness and crispness of structure cause it to rot quicker than the old green kinds; but for use during the months of October, November, December, and the early part of January, I advise it to be grown, if the saving of labor and quality be considerations. It is equally as hardy against frost as the other kinds. In size and weight it is very similar to those popular kinds, the "Golden Dwarf" and "Half Dwarf;" in fact, it originated in what is known as a "sport" from the "Half Dwarf;" that is, a single plant showed the whiteness of stem and peculiar feathery leaves, which, fortunately, were permanently reproduced from seed, and gave us this entirely new type of Celery. Its culture is in all respects the same as that directed for the other sorts, with the exception that we are saved the trouble of high "banking."

Last season a few thousand bunches were sold for the first time in the New York markets, and were quickly disposed of at nearly double the price of the ordinary sorts of the same size. It was purchased exclusively by the purveyors for the leading hotels, and, from its beautiful appearance, created an interest in this vegetable which never had been shown before. Its only drawback, as I have said, is that, from its tenderness, it will not keep as well into late winter as the green sorts; but as it can be had in perfection through the Christmas holidays, the time when Celery is in greater demand than at any other season, it will without doubt at once be largely grown, and grown to supply the holiday demand, to the exclusion of all other kinds.

STRAWBERRY CULTURE.

Our system of growing Strawberries from pot layers has now extended all over the country, and particularly in the Eastern and Middle States. There is no question that it is by far the most simple and satisfactory for private use, if it is not also for market.

Strawberries will grow on almost any soil, but it is all-important that it be well drained, either naturally or artificially; in fact, this is true for the well-being of nearly all plants, as few do well on soils where the water does not freely pass off.

Thorough culture requires that the soil should be first dug or plowed, then spread over with at least three inches of thoroughly rotted stable manure, which should be dug or plowed under, so far as practicable, to mix it with the soil. If stable manure cannot be had, artificial manure, such as bone dust, etc., should be sown on the dug or plowed ground, thick enough to nearly cover it, then harrowed or chopped in with a fork, so that it is well mixed with the soil to at least six inches in depth. This, then, is the preliminary work before planting, to insure a crop the next season after planting, or in nine or ten months.

Pot Layers.

The plants must be such as are *layered in pots*, and the sooner they are planted out after the 15th of July, the better, although, if not then convenient, they will produce a crop the next season, even if planted as late as the middle of September; but the sooner they are planted the larger will be the crop. They may be set from *pot layers* either in beds of four rows each, fifteen inches apart, and fifteen inches between the plants, leaving two feet between the beds for pathway; or be set out in rows two feet apart, the plants in the rows fifteen inches apart; and if the plants are properly set out, (care being taken to firm the soil around the plant, which is best done by pressing the soil against each plant with the foot,) not one plant in a thousand of Strawberry plants that have been grown in pots will fail to grow.

For the first three or four weeks after planting nothing need be done except to hoe the beds, so that all weeds are kept down. Be careful to do this once in every ten days; for if the weeds once get a start, it will treble the labor of keeping the ground clean. If Strawberries are grown on a large scale, by all means use a wheel hoe, such as the "Gem" or "Universal," which will save four-fifths of the labor of hoeing, and do the work better. In about a month after planting they will begin to throw out runners, all of which *must be pinched or cut off as they appear*, so that by the end of the growing season (1st of November) each plant will have formed a complete bush one foot or more in diameter, having the necessary matured "crowns" for next June's fruit.

MULCHING.

By the middle of December the entire beds of Strawberry plants should be covered up with salt-meadow hay (straw, leaves, or anything similar will do as well) to the depth of two or three inches, entirely covering up the plants and soil, so that nothing is seen but the hay. By April, the plants so protected will show indications of

STRAWBERRY CULTURE.

growth, when the hay around each plant is pushed a little aside, to assist it in getting through the covering, so that by May the fully developed plant shows on the clean surface of the hay. This *mulching*, as it is called, is indispensable to the best culture, as it protects the plants from cold in winter, keeps the fruit clean, keeps the roots cool by shading them from the hot sun in June, and at the same time saves nearly all further labor after being once put on, as few weeds can push through it.

NEW BEDS EVERY YEAR.

By this method I prefer to plant *new beds every year*, though, if desired, the beds once planted may be fruited for two or three years, as by the old plans; but the fruit the first season will always be the largest in size, if not greatest in number. Another advantage of this system is that, where space is limited, there is quite time enough to get a crop of Potatoes, Pease, Beans, Lettuce, Radishes, or, in fact, any summer crop off the ground first *before* planting the Strawberries, thus taking two crops from the ground in one year, if desired, and there is also plenty of time to crop the ground with Cabbage, Cauliflower, Celery, or other fall crop *after* the crop of Strawberries has been gathered.

HOW TO MAKE POT LAYERS.

The plan of getting the pot layers of Strawberries is very simple. Just as soon as the fruit is gathered, if the beds are well forked up or deeply cultivated by a wheel hoe between the rows, the runners or young plants will begin to grow, and in two weeks will be fit to layer in pots. The pots, which should be from two to three inches in diameter, are filled with the soil in which the Strawberries are growing, and "plunged" or sunk to the level of the surface; the Strawberry layer is then laid on the pot, and held in place with a small stone. The stone not only serves to keep the plant in its place, so that its roots will strike into the pot, but it also serves to mark where each pot is; for, being sunk to the level of the surface, rains wash the soil around the pots, so that they could not well be seen unless marked by the stone.

In ten or twelve days after the Strawberry layers have been put down the pots will be filled with roots. They are then cut from the parent plant, placed closely together, and shaded and watered for a few days before being planted out. Some plant them out at once when taken up, but, unless the weather is very suitable, some loss may occur by this method; by the other plan, however, of hardening them for a few days, not one in a thousand will fail.

I find that in hot, dry weather it is of great benefit to plants newly planted to place along each side of them a mulch of either rough manure, dried grass from the lawn that has been cut by the mowing machine, or any such material that will act as a non-conductor, so as to prevent the rays of the hot sun striking down on and drying and heating up the bare soil. If properly planted and mulched by some such material, no water need ever be used in the hottest or driest weather.

I planted out on the 15th of August the past season over ten thousand pot-grown Strawberry plants, mulched them in this way with dried grass cut by machine from the lawn, and, although we gave no water, and had not a drop of rain for thirty days, yet nearly every plant has made a growth that is certain to give a full crop of Strawberries next season, as at present date of writing

(November 1st) the plants set out in August are nine inches in diameter, with three to six crowns. This mulching after planting is equally beneficial to Celery or any other crop that it is necessary to plant during the hot and dry months of July, August, and September.

Field Culture.

Strawberries for field culture are usually planted from the ordinary layers, either in August and September in the fall, or in March, April, or May in the spring. They are usually planted in rows, two to three feet apart, and nine to twelve inches between the plants. In planting, every plant should be well firmed,.or great loss is almost certain to ensue, as the Strawberry is a plant always difficult to transplant. They are usually worked by a horse cultivator, and generally two or three crops are taken before the beds are plowed under; but the first crop given (which is in the second year after planting) is always the best. The same care must be taken as in planting by pot layers, the ground kept clear of weeds, and the runners pinched or cut off to make fruiting crowns.

By the usual field method of culture, it will be seen that there is a loss of one season in about three; for in the year of planting no fruit, of course, is produced, and for this reason I incline to the belief that, if a portion were set aside to produce early plants, so that pot layers could be set out by the 15th of July, a full crop of the finest fruit could be had every season, and with less cost, I think; for the only labor after planting is to keep the ground clean and pinch off the runners, from July to October, with the certainty of getting a full crop next June, or in less than a year from the time of planting, while by planting by ordinary layers, if planted in

August, we have three months of fall culture, and six or seven months of the next summer's culture, before a crop is produced. Again, if the crop is continued to fruit the second or third year, every one who has had experience with the nature of the plant, knows that the labor of keeping the plants free from weeds is enormous; while by the pot layering method of taking a fresh crop each year, all such labor is dispensed with.

KINDS OF STRAWBERRIES.

Although it is difficult to give any list of kinds of Strawberries that will do well under all conditions, yet, taking the suburbs of New York as a standard, (which, with its great variety of soil, is likely to be as good as any other,) I find that the best ten kinds, having the greatest combination of good qualities, that I can select from a collection of fifty leading sorts, are the following, which are named in the order of their excellence :

JERSEY QUEEN.— This variety was sold for the first time in the fall of 1881, and is, in my opinion, unequaled by any variety of Strawberry thus far introduced. The size is immense, often measuring six inches in circumference. Shape, roundish conical; color, a beautiful scarlet crimson; perfectly solid, and of excellent flavor. It is an immense bearer, many plants averaging a quart of first quality fruit. It is one of the latest,

JERSEY QUEEN.

the crop in this vicinity being in perfection about the 25th of June, while the average crop of Strawberries is at its best by the 15th of June in the locality of New York.

LONGFELLOW IMPROVED.—A seedling raised by a blacksmith named Adams, of Hudson County, New Jersey. It is the most beautiful Strawberry I have ever seen. It was admired as the finest in the exhibit of over two hundred sorts at the New York Horticultural Society's rooms in June of 1883. It is of the largest size; a dark, glossy crimson, with prominent golden seeds, and of excellent flavor.

PRINCE OF BERRIES.—A seedling of Mr. Durand's, who has never introduced anything that has not proved good. This one is of large size, deep crimson color, and of excellent flavor.

BIDWELL.—One of the very best, abundantly productive, large size, excellent flavor, and one of the very earliest. Plants set out from pot layers on August 5th, 1880, had fruit ripe June 5th, 1881, ten months from date of planting. The plants averaged one quart of fruit each. There is one fault of the Bidwell; it is so enormously productive, that if the soil is poor half of the berries often fail to mature.

NECTAR.—Another new kind that will be offered for the first time this year, (1884.) It is of fine appearance, full average size, and a richness of flavor surpassing anything yet in cultivation.

SHARPLESS.—With the exception of Jersey Queen, the largest and one of the heaviest berries of this collection. It is of fine flavor, a good bearer, and has now become a standard sort.

JUCUNDA.—This is an old, well-known sort, possessing so many good qualities, that I place it as one of the best ten in preference to scores of others of later origin. It is of full average size, wonderfully productive, of great beauty of color and form, and excellent flavor; but its distinctive value is in its ripening, extending from the earliest to the latest season of the crop, the first berries being ripe here about June 4th, and extending unto July 4th. In some soils it is rather a weak grower.

DOWNING.—One of the best of the older sorts, combining all the best qualities, being large, early, rich in color and flavor, and abundantly productive.

MANCHESTER.—A new variety introduced in 1882. It is a most abundant bearer, of good size and fair flavor, and will likely prove a good market sort.

MANCHESTER.

GLOSSY CONE.—Although this has been grown by the raiser, Mr. Durand, for many years, it was issued first in 1881. In a test of fifty kinds in our grounds, I found it the earliest of all, except Bidwell, very prolific, of good size, fine flavor, and altogether has a combination of good qualities rarely found in any *early* Strawberry. Its only fault is, that it is rather a weak grower, and requires a rich and rather heavy soil to develop its best qualities.

I am often asked the number of Strawberry plants that it is necessary to plant for the use of a private family. The best answer to this is to state that, under ordinary culture by the pot layer plant, one hundred plants will give twenty-five quarts. The crop runs over a period of from twelve to fifteen days, so that purchasers with this knowledge will be the best judges of the number needed.

ROOT CROPS

FOR

FARM STOCK.

BY PETER HENDERSON.

(From the American Agriculturist of April, 1878.)

WHILE "Mangels" and other roots for stock feeding have been largely cultivated in Europe for the past fifty years, it is surprising how little it is yet done here, particularly when we know how well our soil and climate are, in most sections, adapted to the purpose, and how great are our necessities, particularly in those States where the long, dry summers diminish the crop of hay and other fodder plants. The most important root crop for stock is the Mangel-wurzel, which, I believe, can be grown and matured in any good soil in any state in the Union. As with all root crops, a loose, friable soil, with a sandy or gravelly subsoil, is better adapted to it than a stiff soil with a clayey subsoil. All root crops require deep culture. The soil should always be plowed to the depth of ten inches, and, if it can be done, it will pay well to let the subsoil plow follow in the wake of the other, and stir the subsoil ten inches more, making a loosened depth of twenty inches.

In many of our deep, rich, new soils an excellent crop of Mangels, or other roots, can be grown without manure; but, when necessary to use it, nothing is better than well-rotted stable manure, composted with as much muck or turf from roadsides, spread evenly over the surface before plowing, at the rate of from six to twelve tons per acre. In the absence of stable manure, bone dust, superphosphate, or guano should be applied, at the rate of from 300 to 500 pounds per acre; but all such concentrated fertilizers should be sown on the surface, after plowing, and harrowed in, until thoroughly mixed with the soil. Before sowing, the ground should be smoothed as evenly as possible with the back of the harrow, to present a smooth and level surface for the reception of the seed.

The distance apart between the rows for Mangels will vary with the character of the soil. In light, sandy soils, the rows should be twenty-four inches apart, with nine inches between the plants; but in strong, rich, deep soils, the rows should be thirty inches apart and twelve inches between the plants. This is what is termed the "flat culture." Mr. Wm. Crozier, of Northport, L. I., works on an entirely different plan from this, and his success in producing enormous crops shows it to be well worthy of imitation. After thoroughly plowing, harrowing, and smoothing the land, he strikes out furrows with the double mould-board plow, (if this is not obtainable, any plow that will make such a furrow will do,) thirty inches apart. The furrow is six to seven inches deep. These furrows are then half filled up with a compost made from stable manure and turf parings from the roadside, about equal parts, thoroughly mixed and decomposed, or, if yet rough and unrotted, it is pressed down in the rows with the feet. After the manure has been thus placed in the furrows, the plow is run up between on each side, so as not only to cover in the manure, but to raise a ridge as high as the furrow was deep. These ridges are now run over with a roller or light chain harrow, so as to take off or flatten down two or three inches of the apex, and so broaden the ridge as to allow the seed sower to work on it to deposit the seed. Where stable manure is not obtainable, Mr. Crozier recommends blood and bone fertilizer, or bone dust, sown in the furrows at the rate of about 300 pounds to the acre; but where such fertilizers are used, the ridge over the furrows should not be raised so high as over the manure. About eight pounds of seed are used to the acre, if put in with the "Planet" or other seed drill; when sown by hand, fully double that quantity would be required per acre. The seed ranges, according to the season and the variety, from forty to eighty cents per pound. Mr. Meggat, the extensive seed raiser of Connecticut, recommends that, in using the seed sower, the hopper should never be more than two-thirds filled, and should never have any lid or cover, so that the operator can see its action, and should be shaken clear of all dust as it accumulates, so that the seed may be

NORBITON GIANT MANGEL WURZEL.

evenly distributed. When the plants are up, they are to be thinned to twelve or fourteen inches apart, and the land is well cultivated, so that, before the crop covers the ground, the ridges have been so leveled down that the rows of roots are nearly as low as the spaces between. The ridge system of culture, both for Mangels and Turnips, although it requires more labor, is a saving in manure, and there is no doubt that these crops are greatly benefited by having the soil gradually taken from the ridge by the cultivator, and exposing their roots, or "bulbs," to the air.

KINVER YELLOW GLOBE MANGEL.

The best time for sowing, in the latitude of New York, is from May 1st to the 15th. The time must, of course, be varied according to locality. Probably the best guide in all sections is to sow from eight to ten days *before* the time that Corn is usually planted. The varieties most used are the "Long Red" and "Norbiton Giant," (red varieties,) and the "Yellow Ovoid" and "New Kinver Globe," both yellow kinds. The average weight of the crop of an acre of Mangels is forty tons; though in some soils they have yielded double that weight. Of course, their cash value, as compared with hay, (rating hay at $15 per ton,) will vary largely under different circumstances, but Mr. William Crozier considers the average value of Mangels, for stock-feeding purposes, to be $4 per ton, or $160 per acre. While hay would be, under the same condition, (estimating two tons per acre,) only worth $30 per acre, the expense of seed, manure, and cultivation of the Mangels, at the utmost, need not exceed $80 per acre; so it is clearly seen that the crop for feeding purposes is a profitable one.

Turnip Culture.

What has been said on the modes of culture for Mangels may be applied to Turnip culture, except as to the time of sowing. The Swedish or Ruta Baga varieties of Turnip should be sown, in this latitude, from May 25th to June 25th, and the Yellow Aberdeen, or strap-leaved kinds, from July 1st to the middle of August. When sown at these dates, the distance apart may be the same as for Mangels, but both of the classes may be sown a month later; that is, the Ruta Bagas may be sown from June 25th to July 25th, and the strap-leaved kinds from the middle of August to the middle of September; but when sown thus late they should be, both between rows and between plants, one-third closer. The varieties that I find best are, "American Ruta Baga" and "Purple-top Ruta Baga;" of the strap-leaved kinds, "Red-top Strap-leaved" and "Yellow Aberdeen." Mr. Crozier's estimate of the value of Ruta Bagas, as compared with hay, (at

$15 per ton,) is $5 per ton; average crop, 25 tons per acre, or $125. Purple-top Strap-leaved or Yellow Aberdeen Turnips he estimates at $3.50 per ton; average crop, 35 tons per acre, or $122.50. Estimating the expense of culture at half the gross value, we have still a large margin in favor of the crop; besides, the strap-leaved Turnips can be sown after Barley, Oats, or Rye.

CARROTS.

Carrots may properly come under the head of "Root Crops for Stock," though mainly grown for horses; but, even for horses, Mr. Crozier says that he considers them far inferior to Ruta Baga Turnips. This is in opposition to the received notion; but we know that public opinion in matters of this sort is often wrong, and when we consider the marked success of Mr. Crozier as a raiser of both horses and cattle, his opinion in this matter is entitled to consideration.

The land for Carrots should be prepared exactly as for Mangels. It must be deeply plowed, harrowed, and thoroughly pulverized, and whatever kind of fertilizing material is used, should be thoroughly mixed with the soil to a depth of at least ten inches. The same quantity and kind of fertilizers should be used as recommended for the flat culture of Mangels, though in new lands, or lands on which Corn has been grown after sod, enough of the fertilizing material will usually be left in the soil to mature a good crop of Carrots without any manure, provided the soil is deep and in good condition. I once grew twenty tons of Carrots per acre on land in this condition, without using a particle of manure. Carrots should be sown from the 1st to the 30th of May, and when sown by a seed drill, about four pounds of seed to the acre are required. The rows should be two feet distant, and the plants thinned out to five or six inches apart. An average crop is fifteen tons, of the "Long Orange" variety, to the acre, and the present price averages $15 per ton in the New York market. The "White" or "Yellow Belgian" Carrots would give one-third more weight, but the quality is inferior and the price correspondingly lower.

Keeping Roots in Winter.

One of the seeming obstacles to raising root crops on a large scale is the lack of a proper place for keeping them in winter. A general impression prevails that they must be kept in cellars or in a root house specially built for the purpose. There is really no necessity for a special root house, as the simple and cheap method of preserving them in pits in the open ground is far better. I will briefly describe my plan, which I have practised with all kinds of market garden roots for twenty-five years. Mangels, in this section of the country, are dug up towards the end of October, or just after our first slight frost. They are then temporarily secured from severe frosts by placing them in convenient oblong heaps, say three feet high by six feet wide, and are covered with three or four inches of soil, which will be sufficient protection for three or four weeks after lifting; by that time, say the end of November, they may be stowed away in their permanent winter quarters. For Turnips and Carrots, there is less necessity for the temporary pitting, as they are much hardier roots, and may be left in the ground until the time necessary for permanent pitting, if time will not permit of securing them temporarily.

The advantage of this temporary pitting is, that it enables them to be quickly secured at a season when work is usually pressing, and allows the period of their permanent pitting to be extended into a comparatively cold season. This is found to be of the utmost importance in preserving all kinds of roots; the same rules regulating the preservation in winter, apply as in spring sowing. While in this section of the country it must be done not later than the end of November, in some of the Southern States the time may be extended a month later, while in places where the thermometer does not fall lower than 25° *above* zero, there is no need to dig up any of these roots at all, as that degree of cold would not injure them.

The permanent pit is made as follows: A piece of ground is chosen where no water will stand in winter. If not naturally drained, provision must be made to carry off the water. The pit is then dug four feet deep and six feet wide, and of any length required. The roots are then evenly packed in sections of about four feet wide, *across* the pit, and only to the height of the ground level. Between the sections a space of half a foot is left, which is filled up with soil level to the top. This gives a section of roots four feet deep and wide, and four feet long, each section divided from the next by six inches of soil, forming a series of small pits, holding from six to twelve barrels of roots, one of which can be taken out without disturbing the next, which is separated from it by six inches of soil.

Scotch Method of Wintering Roots.

Mr. Crozier practises, with great success, the Scotch method of preserving root crops in winter, which he thus describes :

A dry spot being selected, where no water will stand in winter, a space is marked out six feet in width, and of any length required. This bed is excavated ten to twelve inches deep, and the soil is thrown out on the bank. The roots, either Mangels, Turnips, Carrots, or Potatoes, are built up evenly to a sharp point about five or six feet in height, so that the roots form almost an equal-sided triangle, six feet on the sides. This bed of roots is then thatched over with four inches of straw, after which the earth is banked over the whole about one foot in thickness. This covering of earth and straw is sufficient to keep out any degree of frost that we have in this latitude, though we rarely have it much below zero. In colder or warmer sections, judgment must be used to increase or lessen the covering. Vents, or chimneys, made by a three-inch drain pipe, or anything of similar size, are placed every six or seven feet along the top of the pit, resting on the roots, so that the moisture generated may escape. In extremely cold weather, these vents or chimneys should be closed up, as the cold might be severe enough to get down to the roots. Pits so constructed rarely fail to preserve roots perfectly until late in spring, and are in every respect preferable to root cellars; for, no matter how cold the weather may be, they are easily got at; the end once opened, the soil forms a frozen arch over the pit. Mr. Crozier says he has practised this plan for years on his farm at Northport, L. I., some of his pits containing hundreds of tons of Mangels, etc.

GARDEN VEGETABLES.

There are a number of *garden vegetables* that can be kept equally well by the same method as that recommended for farm roots. The only difference would be, that the pits may be made somewhat narrower, so as to accommodate less quantities. Although such crops as Parsnips, Salsify, and Horseradish are entirely hardy, yet, as it is often impossible to get into the ground to dig them in winter, all that are wanted for use before spring opens should be dug up in November, and pitted in the manner above described.

It is important that these hardy roots be not dug too early, else they will lose their color and flavor; consequently, digging should be delayed as long as the frost will permit. It is a good plan, if litter or leaves are convenient, to use them for covering the ground where the roots are growing three or four inches, so as to protect the roots against freezing, thus often extending the period of digging these hardy roots to the middle of December. When in the market garden business we often covered over as much as five acres in this way, which well repaid the labor by the improved condition of the roots, as frequently an advance of 25 per cent. in price was obtained by a superior color and flavor.

CULTURE

OF

ALFALFA OR LUCERNE,

(*Medicago sativa.*)

(Written by Peter Henderson for the United States Agricultural Report for 1884.)

IN a country so wide spread and diversified as the United States, it is not to be wondered at that a crop that is valued in some localities is unknown in others. But it is somewhat surprising that, in many of the Southern States, where the want of forage is so much felt, the culture of a plant so admirably adapted for their soil and climate has so long been neglected. In a visit to Florida in February, 1883, I was impressed, as every Northern man must be, with the utter dearth of forage plants, and, as a consequence, the hungry and meager, starved-looking cattle. To my inquiries everywhere, the same reply was given, that no good grass or clover could be found to stand the heat and drought of their long summers. Fortunately, in alluding to the subject, while in the company of Mr. R. Bronson, of St. Augustine, Florida, he promptly showed a practical solution of the difficulty, by taking me to a patch of Alfalfa, about twenty-five feet by one hundred, or only about the one-sixteenth part of an acre. From that little patch, Mr. B. assured me that he had fed a cow during the summer months, getting as fine milk and butter as he ever got North; and further said that twice that area, or one-eighth part of an acre, would be ample to supply a cow with food during the entire season.

The land used by Mr. Bronson for his experiment with Alfalfa was identical with the thousands of acres in his immediate vicinity, which was given over to the Blue Palmetto and scrubby pines, through which the goat-like cattle browse out a miserable existence. Mr. Bronson, though only an amateur, is a careful observer, and an enthusiastic student in everything that relates to agriculture. In the culture of Alfalfa for Florida and other Southern latitudes, he advises that the crop be sown early in the fall; early enough to attain a height of four or five inches before growth is arrested by cold weather; in Florida say from the 1st to the 15th of October.

The soil best suited for the growth of Alfalfa is that which is deep and sandy; hence the soil of Florida and many other portions of the cotton belt are eminently fitted for it. The plant makes a tap root with few laterals, and its roots are often found at a depth of six to eight feet, thus drawing food from depths entirely beyond the action of drought or heat. When Alfalfa is to be grown on a large scale, to get at the best results, the ground chosen should be high and level, or, if not high, such as is entirely free from under water. Drainage must be as near perfect as possible, either naturally or artificially. This, in fact, is a primary necessity for *every* crop, unless it be such as is aquatic or sub-aquatic.

Deep plowing, thorough harrowing and leveling with that valuable implement, the "smoothing harrow," to get a smooth and level surface, are the next operations. This should be done, in the Southern States, from the 1st to the 20th of October, or at such season in the fall as would be soon enough to insure a growth of four or five inches before the season of growth stops. Draw out lines on the prepared land twenty inches apart, (if for horse culture, but if for hand culture, fourteen inches,) and two or three inches deep. These lines are best made by what market gardeners call a "marker," which is made by nailing six tooth-shaped pickets six or eight inches long, at the required distance apart, to a three by four inch joist, to which a handle is attached, which makes the marker or drag. The first tooth is set against a garden line drawn tight across the field; the marker is dragged backward by the workman, each tooth marking a line. Thus the six teeth mark six lines, if the line is set each time; but it is best to place the end tooth of the marker in a line already made, so that in this way only five lines are marked at once; but it is quicker to do this than move the line.

The lines being marked out, the seed is sown by hand or by seed-drill, at the rate of eight to twelve pounds per acre. (The price ranges from thirty to fifty cents per pound.) After sowing, (and this rule applies to all seeds, if sown by hand,) *the seed must be trodden in by walking on the lines, so as to press the seed down into the drills.* After treading in, the ground must be leveled by raking with a wooden or steel rake along the lines lengthways, not across. That done, it would be advantageous to use a roller over the land, so as to smooth the surface and further firm the seed; but this is not indispensable. When seeds are drilled in by a machine, the wheel presses down the soil on the seeds, so that treading in with the feet is not necessary.

After the seeds germinate so as to show the rows, which will be in from two to four weeks, according to the weather, the ground must be hoed between, and this is best done by some light wheel hoe, if by hand, such as the "Universal." On light, sandy soil, such as in Florida, a man could with ease run over two to three acres per day. The labor entailed in this method of sowing Alfalfa in drills is somewhat greater than when sown broadcast in the usual way of grasses and clover, but there is no question that it is by far the best and most profitable plan, for it must be remembered that the plant is a *hardy perennial*, and is good for a crop for eight to ten years. Moreover, the sowing in drills admits of the crop being easily fertilized, if it is found necessary to do so; as all that is necessary is to sow bone dust, superphosphates, or other concentrated fertilizer between the rows, and then stir it into the soil by the use of the wheel hoe. In the ground of Mr. Bronson, of St. Augustine, Florida, he found that the seed sown in the middle of October gave him a crop fit to cut in three months after sowing; and three heavy crops after, during the same year; and I have little doubt that in that climate and soil, so congenial to its growth, six heavy green crops could be cut annually, after the plant is fairly established, if a moderate amount of fertilizer were used, say 300 pounds of superphosphate or bone dust to the acre.

Mr. William Crozier, of Northport, L. I., one of the best known farmers and stock breeders in the vicinity of New York, says that he has long considered Alfalfa one of the best forage crops. He uses it always to feed his milch cows and breeding ewes, particularly in preparing them for exhibition at fairs, where he is known to be a most successful competitor, and always takes along sufficient Alfalfa hay to feed them on while there. Mr. Crozier's system of culture is broadcast, and he uses some fifteen or sixteen pounds of seed to the acre; but his land is unusually clean and in a high state of cultivation, which enables him to adopt the broadcast plan; but on the average land it will be found that the plan of sowing in drills would be the best.

Mr. Crozier's crop, the second year, averaged eighteen tons green to the acre, and about six tons when dried as hay. For his section (the latitude of New York) he finds the best date of sowing is the first week in May, and a good cutting can be had in September. The next season a full crop is obtained, when it is cut, if green, three or four times. If to be used for hay, it is cut in the condition of ordinary Red Clover, in blossom. It then makes after that two green crops if cut; and sometimes the last one, instead of being cut, is fed on the ground by sheep or cattle.

Mr. E. M. Sargent, Macon, Georgia, writing to me under date March 6th, 1883, says: " I consider Alfalfa to be the most valuable forage plant that can be used in this section of the country; that is, the entire cotton belt, or north of it, if the land is sandy without a clay subsoil too near the surface. Planters are just beginning to find out its merits; and no poverty of stock will ever occur where Alfalfa is raised. In the summer of 1881, when everything else was parched here with heat and drought, this alone was prompt in its maturity for the mower. It should be cut for hay when in blossom, and can easily be cut three or four times here wherever the land is in fairly good condition.

" Those who *do not* succeed with it, sow it broadcast and surrender it to the hogs early in the season. Those who do succeed, sow in drills eighteen inches apart and cultivate early."

It will be seen that Mr. Sargent advises drills much wider than I recommend, which I presume is to admit the horse hoe, but a quicker crop undoubtedly would be got at fourteen inches apart; and by use of the hand

"Universal Wheel Hoe," the work could be done on light soil nearly as quickly as by the horse cultivator.

Alfalfa is extensively grown in Europe, particularly in France and Germany, where it is considered a valuable crop for rotation, and is classed by the French as one of the *plantes ameliorantes;* for in southern France Wheat has been successfully raised after six or seven years of Alfalfa on ground which formerly had failed to give good crops of Wheat. Although Alfalfa may be grown in cold latitudes as well as in warm, as the plant is entirely hardy, yet its value is not so marked in cold climates, where it finds competitors in Red Clover and the grasses; but in light soils anywhere, particularly in warm climates, its deep-rooting properties make it comparatively independent of moisture; hence it is the forage plant *par excellence* for the Southern States, wherever the soil is light and sandy; but it should never be grown on stiff soils, for, unless the roots can penetrate deeply, good results cannot be expected. When it is considered that immense sums are paid annually for baled hay by the Southern to the Northern States, the wonder is how long they will continue to do so, with the material at hand to produce a better article at probably one-fourth the cost.

At the date of this writing, thousands in Florida and other Southern States are engaged in the culture of Oranges and other fruits, as well as vegetables, for the Northern markets; and while in specially favored locations success has attended these enterprises, yet it is doubtful if one in four makes it profitable; while, with the culture of this valuable forage plant, the vast sums paid for northern hay would not only be saved, but the products of the dairy would assume an importance which now, among most farmers in the extreme Southern States, is altogether unknown.

MANURES

AND

THEIR MODES OF APPLICATION.

The subject of Manures is one of the greatest importance to every operator in the soil, whether farmer, market gardener, florist, or such as cultivate only for their own use, for under few conditions can crops be long grown without the use of fertilizers. Although I have already given general instructions about fertilizers in all my works on gardening, yet I find, from the number of inquiries received from even such as have my works, that the matter has not been there treated sufficiently in detail to meet the wants of the varied conditions under which the necessity for the use of fertilizers arises.

The comparative value of manures must be regulated by the cost; for example, if rotted Stable Manure, whether from horses or cows, can be delivered on the ground at $3 per ton, it is about as valuable, for fertilizing purposes, as Peruvian Guano at $65 per ton, or pure Bone Dust at $40 per ton, and is better than either of these, or any other concentrated fertilizer, from the fact of its mechanical action on the land, that is, its assistance, from its light, porous nature, in aerating and pulverizing the soil; Guano, Bone Dust, or other commercial fertilizers, acting only as such, without in any way assisting to make better what may be called the physical condition of the soil.

All experienced cultivators know that the first year that land is broken up from sod, if proper culture has been given, by thorough plowing and harrowing, (provided the land is drained artificially or naturally, so as to be free from water, and relieve it from "sourness,") the land is in better condition for any crop, than land that has been continuously cropped without a rest. The market gardeners in the vicinity of New York are now so well convinced of this that, when twenty acres are under cultivation, at least five acres are continually kept in grain, clover, and grass, to be broken up successively, every second or third year, so as to get the land in the condition that nothing else but rotted, pulverized sod will accomplish. This is done in cases where land is as valuable as $500 per acre; experience having proved that, with one-quarter of the land "resting under grass," more profit can be got than if the whole were under culture.

When the rotation, by placing a portion of the land under grass, cannot be done, then it is absolutely necessary to use Stable Manure, at least to some extent, if the best results are desired, for continuous cropping of the soil. Where concentrated fertilizers only are used, they will not continue to give satisfactory results after the grass roots, or other organic matter, have passed from the soil, all of which will usually be entirely gone by the third or fourth year after breaking up. I have long held the opinion, that the idea of lands having been permanently exhausted by tobacco or other crops is a fallacy. What gives rise to this belief, I think, is the fact that, when lands are first broken up from the forest or meadow lands, for three or four years the organic matter in the soil, (the roots of grasses, leaves, etc.,) not only serves to feed the crops, but it keeps the soil in a better state of pulverization, or what might be called aerated condition, than when, in the course of cropping for a few years, it has passed away. Stable Manure best supplies this want; but on farm lands away from towns, it is not often that enough can be obtained to have any appreciable effect on the soil, and hence artificial fertilizers are resorted to, which often fail, not from any fault in themselves, but from the fact that, exerting little mechanical influence on the land, it becomes compacted or sodden, the air cannot get to the roots, and hence failure or partial failure of crop.

Thus, we see, that to have the best results from commercial fertilizers, it is of great importance to have the land "rested" by a crop of grain or grass every three or four years.

The best known fertilizers of commerce are Peruvian Guano and Bone Dust, though there are numbers of others, such as Fish Guano, Dry Blood Fertilizer, Blood and Bone Fertilizer, with the various brands of superphosphates, all of more or less value for fertilizing purposes. It is useless to go over the list, and we will confine ourselves to the relative merits of pure Peruvian Guano and pure Bone Dust. Guano, at $65 per ton, we consider relatively equal in value to Bone Dust at $40 per ton, for in the lower-priced article we find we have to increase the quantity to produce the same results. Whatever kind of concentrated fertilizer is used, we find it well repays the labor to prepare it in the following manner before it is used on the land:

To every bushel of Guano or Bone Dust add three bushels of either leaf mould, (from the woods,) well-pulverized dry muck, sweepings from a paved street, Stable Manure so rotted as to be like pulverized muck, or, if neither of these can be obtained, any loamy soil will do; but in every case the material to mix the fertilizers with must be fairly dry and never in a condition of mud; the meaning of the operation being, that the material used is to act as a temporary absorbent for the fertilizer. The compost must be thoroughly mixed, and if Guano is used, it being sometimes lumpy, it must be broken up to dust before being mixed with the absorbent.

The main object of this operation is for the better separation and division of the fertilizer, so that, when applied to the soil, it can be more readily distributed. My experiments have repeatedly shown that this method of using concentrated fertilizers materially increases their value, probably twenty per cent. The mixing should be done a few months previous to spring, and it should, after being mixed, be packed away in barrels, and kept in some dry shed or cellar until wanted for use. Thus mixed, it is particularly beneficial on lawns or other grass lands. The quantity of concentrated fertilizer to be used is often perplexing to beginners. I give the following as the best rules I know, all derived from my own practice in growing fruits, flowers, and vegetables:

Taking Guano as a basis, I would recommend for all vegetable or fruit crops, if earliness and good quality are desired, the use of not less than 1,200 pounds per acre, (an acre contains 4,840 square yards, and cultivators for private use can easily estimate from this the quantity they require for any area,) mixed with two tons of either of the materials before recommended. If Bone Dust is used, about one ton per acre should be applied, mixed with three tons of soil or the other materials named.

For market garden vegetable crops, in the vicinity of New York, this quantity of Guano or Bone Dust is harrowed in after twenty-five or thirty tons of Stable Manure have first been plowed in; so that the actual cost of manuring each acre is not less than $100, and often $150.

When fertilizers are used alone, without being mixed with the absorbent, they should be sown on the soil after plowing or digging, about thick enough to just color the surface, or about as thick as sand or sawdust is sown on a floor, and then thoroughly harrowed in if plowed, or, if dug, chopped in with a rake. This quantity is used broadcast by sowing on the ground after plowing, and deeply and thoroughly harrowing in, or, if in small gardens, forked in lightly with the prongs of a garden fork or long-toothed steel rake. When applied in hills or drills, from 100 to 300 pounds should be used to the acre, according to the distance of these apart, mixing with soil, etc., as already directed.

When well-rotted Stable Manure is procurable at a cost not to exceed $3 per ton, delivered on the ground, whether from horses or cows, it is preferable to any concentrated fertilizer. Rotted Stable Manure, to produce full crops, should be spread on the ground not less than three inches thick, (our market gardeners use from 50 to 75 tons of well-rotted Stable Manure per acre, when no concentrated fertilizer is used,) and should be thoroughly mixed with the soil by plowing or spading. The refuse hops from breweries form an excellent fertilizer, at least one-half more valuable, bulk for bulk, than Stable Manure. Other excellent fertilizers are obtained from the scrapings or shavings from horn or whalebone manufactories. The best way to make these quickly available is to compost them with hot manure, in the proportion of one ton of refuse horn or whalebone with fifteen tons of manure. The heated manure extracts the oil, which is intermingled with the whole.

The manure from the chicken or pigeon house is very valuable, and when composted as directed for Bone Dust and Guano, has at least one-third their value. Castor Oil Pomace is also valuable in about the same proportion.

Poudrette is the name given to a commercial fertilizer,

the composition of which is night soil and dried swamp muck or charcoal dust as an absorbent. It is sold at about $12 to $15 per ton, and at that price may be equal in value, if too much of the absorbing material is not used, to Bone Dust at $40 per ton.

In my early experience as a market gardener, I used large quantities of Night Soil for vegetable crops with the very best results. It was mixed with Stable Manure at the rate of about one ton of Night Soil to fifteen tons of Stable Manure, and put on the land, so mixed, at the rate of 25 tons per acre. In the absence of Stable Manure, dry soil, charcoal dust, sawdust, or any material that will absorb it, will do. Thus mixed, if equal quantities of each have been used, ten tons may be used per acre, if plowed in; if sowed on top, to be harrowed in, say five tons.

Salt has little or no value as a fertilizer, except as a medium of absorbing moisture; for experience shows that soils impregnated by a saline atmosphere are no more fertile than those inland, out of the reach of such an atmosphere.

Muck is the name given to a deposit usually largely composed of vegetable matter, found in swamps or in hollows in forest lands. Of itself it has usually but little fertilizing property, but from its porous nature, when dry, it is one of the best materials to use to mix with other manures as an absorbent. It can be used to great advantage if dug out in winter and piled up in narrow ridges, so that it can be partly dried and "sweetened" in summer. Thus dry, if mixed with Stable Manure, or, better yet, thrown in layers three or four inches thick in the cattle or hog yard, where it can be trodden down and amalgamated with the manure, the value of the manure thus treated will be nearly doubled.

In reply to questions that I receive by the hundred each season, asking whether or not it is worth while to use the so-called special fertilizers, claimed to be suited to the wants of particular plants, such as the "Potato Fertilizer," "Cabbage Fertilizer," "Strawberry Fertilizer," "Rose Fertilizer," etc., I can only give this general answer, that while these manures may suit the plants they are claimed to be "special" for, I have no doubt that either one would suit equally well for the others; or, if all were mixed together, the mixture would be found to answer the purpose for each kind of crop, just as well as if kept separate and applied to the crop it was named for. These hair-splitting distinctions are not recognized to be of any value by one practical farmer or gardener in every hundred; for a little experience soon shows that pure Bone Dust or well-rotted Stable Manure answers for *all* crops alike, no matter what they are. These special fertilizers for special crops are gradually increasing in number, so that some dealers now offer fifty kinds, different brands being offered for plants belonging to the same family. There is an ignorant assumption in this, and any cultivator of ordinary intelligence cannot fail to see that the motive in so doing is to strike as broad a swath as possible, so that a larger number of customers may be reached.

One of my neighbors called the other day, and informed me that his Lettuce crop, in his green-house, was failing, and asked me what I thought of the Lettuce Fertilizer that was offered in a circular that contained some fifty other "specials." An inquiry developed the fact that he had been keeping his Lettuce crop at a night temperature of 65° in January, so that there was just about as much chance of the Special Lettuce Fertilizer helping the crop as there would be of giving health to a man by feeding him beefsteak in the last stages of consumption.

I merely mention this incident to show how, and in what manner, the sellers of these special fertilizers obtain customers.

MARKET GARDENING AROUND NEW YORK.

BY PETER HENDERSON.

(Read before the Annual Meeting of the National Association of Nurserymen, Florists, and Seedsmen, held at Dayton, Ohio, June 16th, 1881.)

PROBABLY nowhere, in this or any other country, is the business of Market Gardening better done than in the vicinity of New York city. The reason for this is probably to be found in the fact, that New York, being the great dépot for all the nationalities of Europe, gets from them the various methods there practised; in addition to this, and what may have even more to do with it, our higher-priced labor forces us to adopt plans entirely unthought of there. Certain it is, that, so far as the practical work in use for cultivation is concerned, our methods, in nearly all operations, are quicker done here than there, and are equally as well done.

In the immediate suburbs of New York, where the lands are rapidly being taken for building sites, many of the market gardeners pay as high as $100 rent per acre annually, and that, too, in most cases, without a lease. All such lands, of course, are cultivated to their fullest capacity, and even at present prices (which are hardly yet up to those of ante-war times) bring an average gross income of about $1,000 per acre.

A great advantage is found in having the lands for growing vegetables as near to the city as possible. The saving in hauling of manure is one important item; but another, and one far more important, is that, if the grower is near enough to the city to make two or three trips a day, in such a fluctuating market as that of New York, it is greatly to his advantage. I have frequently seen that nearly double value could be obtained for products within twenty-four hours. I remember, on one occasion, when engaged in business in Jersey City, where we were within half an hour's time of the great wholesale Washington Market of New York, one Saturday, that each of our four wagons made three trips, taking in twelve loads of Cabbages, which averaged $50 per load; while on the Monday following the same loads only brought us $30 per load. Had we been ten or twelve miles distant from the market, as the greater number of those engaged in the business are, the high rates ruling that day could not have been taken advantage of. I am inclined to believe that, whatever kind of horticultural product is grown, whether fruit, flowers, or vegetables, he that is nearest market, other things being equal, has a decided advantage; so much so that, in most cases, a man had better pay $50 or even $100 per acre rent, if within one or two miles from the market of a large city, than to get land ten or twelve miles away for nothing.

I have little to relate that is new in methods of culture, in the open ground, in market gardening. Nearly the same processes are now practised as when I first wrote my work on this subject in 1866; but since that time we have made many important improvements in culture under glass, particularly in the methods in use in starting plants of Cabbage, Cauliflower, and Lettuce. The old plan of sowing the seeds for these plants in the open air in September, and pricking them off in October, and keeping them in cold frames, is gradually giving way to sowing in green-houses or hot-beds in February, and pricking out in March, which gives a far healthier and nearly as strong a plant, by the first week in April, as those that have been wintered over. The past season we raised nearly half a million of plants in this manner, which we sold at $5 per thousand, a price as profitable to us as the plants were satisfactory to the buyers. We sowed the seed the first week in February, in one of our green-house benches, so thick that they stood twenty plants to the square inch. These we began to thin out, to prick in hot-beds, just as the first rough leaf appeared, placing a thousand plants in a 3×6 sash.

The handling of that quantity was a big job, but I doubt if one plant in a thousand failed, owing, I think, to a plan we used in preparing the bed on the green-house bench for the seeds; a plan that I think well worthy of imitation in preparing a bed for seeds, that have to be transplanted, of any kind, whether outside or under glass. We used only two inches in depth of "soil" for our seed-bed, which was made up as follows: For the first layer, about an inch, we used a good friable loam, run through a half-inch sieve. This was patted down with a spade, and made perfectly level and moderately firm. On this was spread about one-fourth of an inch of Sphagnum, (moss from the swamps,) which had been dried and run through a sieve nearly as fine as mosquito wire, so that it was of the condition of fine sawdust. On the top of the moss the ordinary soil was again strewn, to a depth of about three-fourths of an inch. This being leveled, the seed were sown very thickly, and then pressed into the soil with a smooth board. On this the fine moss was again sifted, thick enough to cover the seed only. The bed was then freely watered with a fine rose, and in a week every seed that had life in it was a plant.

Now this seems a long story to tell about what most

consider a very simple operation, but it is necessary to give these details for a thorough understanding of the advantages of the method. When the seeds of most plants germinate, where they are thickly sown, the stem strikes down into the soil, the roots forming a tap-root with few fibers, unless arrested by something. Here comes the value of our one-fourth of an inch of sifted moss, placed three-quarters of an inch from the top. As soon as the rootlets touch the moss they ramify in all directions, so that when a bunch of seedlings is lifted up and pulled apart, there is a mass of rootlets, to which the moss, less or more, adheres, attached to each. To the practical gardener, the advantage of this is obvious: the tiny seedling has at the start a mass of rootlets ready to work, which strike into the soil at once.

The advantage of the moss covering of the seed is not so apparent, in the matter of a free germinating seed, such as Cabbage, as in many others, but in many families of plants it is of the greatest value. For example, last November I took two lots of ten thousand seeds of Centaurea candida, (one of the Dusty Miller plants so much used for ribbon lines;) both were sown on the same day, and exactly in the same manner, in boxes two inches deep filled with soil; but the one lot was covered with the sifted moss, and the other with fine soil. From the moss-covered lot I got over nine thousand fine plants, while from that covered by soil only about three thousand. The same results were shown in a large lot of seeds of the now famous climbing plant, Ampelopsis Veitchii, and in the finer varieties of Clematis. The dust from Cocoanut fiber will answer the purpose even better than sifted moss, when it can be obtained. The reason is plain: the thin layer of sifted moss never bakes or hardens, holding just the right degree of moisture, and has less tendency to generate damp or fungus than any substance that I know of.

In this connection, I may state that the use of wintered over Lettuce plants, for forcing in green-houses or hothouses, is here, to a great extent, being abandoned, and that the plants used for that purpose are such as have been sown five or six weeks only previous to planting, in the manner described for Cabbage plants, sowings being made for succession, as required. These young plants are found to be far less liable to the Lettuce disease, known as "rust" or "blight," which has created so much havoc in forcing this vegetable in all quarters of the country. I have been written to by hundreds in relation to a remedy for this disease, but know of none, except the use of young plants raised as above recommended, using, wherever practicable, fresh soil each season. One of my neighbors, who uses nearly 3,000 sashes in the forcing of Lettuce, has adopted this plan for the past two years, and has had no Lettuce disease.

As I have before said, although there is but little in general culture to tell, almost every year brings out some improvement in varieties. Within the past dozen years many important advances have been made in earliness and in quality of vegetables. Among Beets, we have the Egyptian, which matures at least five days before any other variety, except the old Bassano, which was too light in color to suit; in Cabbages, the Early Summer; in Cauliflower, the Snowball; in Celery, the Golden Dwarf; and a great improvement has been developed in the White Walnut, a solid, stout kind, with a rich, walnut-like flavor, and graceful, feather-like foliage ; while the new "White Plume" combines the rare qualities of a rich, walnut-like flavor, self-blanching, and a beautiful, plume-like foliage that gives it its name. See page 165.

In Lettuce, the Black-seeded Simpson, the White Summer Cabbage, and the Salamander now lead all the outdoor varieties; in Muskmelons, the Hackensack, of which many thousands of acres are grown for the New York market, is almost exclusively planted. In Pease, a great improvement is developed in the dwarf variety known as American Wonder, though for general early crop the Improved Dan O'Rourke is best. Potatoes vary so much in different localities, that it is difficult to say which of the new sorts are most valued. We find, however, that in our general trade more of Beauty of Hebron is planted than any other of the new sorts. In Radishes, the new Round Dark Red is now the main favorite, while next in order comes the "White-tipped Scarlet Turnip." In Spinach, the Savoy and the new Thick Leaved are the best for general crop; though we find that the Savoy should not be sown in spring, as it runs too quickly to seed. Though every year brings out new claimants for favor in Tomatoes, it is my conviction that we have not advanced one day in earliness (unless in such varieties as Keyes's Prolific and Little Gem, which are of poor quality) in twenty-five years, although we have now many varieties somewhat improved in quality. The varieties now most popular with New York market gardeners are Acme and Paragon, though, from the unusual advertising given to the Trophy, the general cultivation of that is greater than any other; but, as it is usually found now, it is far inferior to many others, besides being one of the latest varieties.

Quite a number of our market gardeners are now getting to grow Strawberries in conjunction with their vegetable crops, by following the pot layering system, by which a crop is obtained in less than a year from the time of planting. We have ourselves grown, for the past six or seven years, upward of an acre of Strawberries in this manner, alternating them with the vegetables grown in our "trial grounds." As the process may be new to some, I will briefly detail it.

Just as soon as the fruit is gathered, the beds are well forked up, and the runners begin to grow rapidly, so that, in the vicinity of New York, we can always obtain strong pot layers by the 10th to the 15th of July. These, if then planted out, never fail (if properly cultivated and the runners kept pinched off) to give a full crop by June of next year; not only a full crop, but finer fruit than is usually obtained by the other methods.

Our manner of performing the operation of layering the runners of Strawberries in pots is as follows: The pots, which should not exceed two and a half inches in diameter, are filled with the soil in which the Strawberries are growing, and "plunged" or sunk to the level of the surface; the Strawberry layer is then laid on the pot, being held in its place with a small stone. The stone not only serves to keep the plant in its place, so that its roots will strike into the soil of the pot, but it also serves to mark where the pot is; for, being sunk to the level of the surface, rains wash the soil around the pots, so that they could not well be seen unless marked by the stone. Any good workman, after a little experience, will layer two thousand per day. In ten or twelve days after the Strawberry layers have been put down, the pots will be filled with roots. They are then cut from the parent plant, taken up, and placed close together, and shaded and watered for a few days before being planted out. If so treated, not one plant in a thousand need fail.

We grow only an acre or so each year, for the purpose of testing varieties; but I am so convinced of the value of the plan, that if I grew largely for market I would prefer it to any other. It will be understood, that by this method the plants only occupy the ground about ten or eleven months, from the time the plants are set out in July or August until the fruit is gathered in June. As I have before said, we alternate the Strawberry crop with vegetables. Our samples of Cabbage, Cauliflower, Radishes, Lettuce, etc., in our trial grounds, occupy the same space, so that when the ground is cleared of these in June or July, the Strawberry layers are planted in their place; while a crop of Celery takes the place of the Strawberry crop that had fruited, so that the ground is never allowed to lie idle.

The question of fertilizers, for the use of the market garden, is now becoming a very serious one for the market gardeners, in such cities as New York, where the manure from the stables does not increase in the ratio of the lands cultivated, as, perhaps, half of all the products grown are shipped to adjacent towns and cities. Still there are few market gardeners who do not use stable manure, which costs, when fit to go on the land, from $2 to $3 per ton. This is put on in spring, at the rate of from fifty to seventy-five tons per acre, which is often supplemented by half a ton of Peruvian Guano or Bone Dust, which is sown on the land and harrowed in, after the stable manure has been plowed in. A great many fertilizers are used besides Peruvian Guano and Bone Dust, such as Fish Guano, Dry Blood Fertilizer, Blood and Bone Fertilizer, together with the various brands of Phosphates; but the majority of cultivators prefer pure Bone Meal or Peruvian Guano to all others.

I saw a list the other day, wherein was enumerated no less than sixteen separate kinds of special fertilizers for thirty different crops, with the chemical elements of each split down to even one-half of one per cent. Now, I know nothing whatever about agricultural chemistry, and it may be presumption in me to criticise such a list; yet when I am told that one kind of fertilizer is needed for Cabbages and another kind for Turnips; one for Sugar Cane and another for Corn; one for Wheat and another for Grass, (plants, if not of the same family, at least of the same natural order,) I am forced to the conclusion that science, so-called, is taking the place of common sense, and is in direct opposition to the experience of the practical farmer or gardener in his operations in the soil.

In our market gardening and green-house operations, we cultivate largely nearly every known family of plants, and in my long experience I have yet to see a fruit, flower, or vegetable crop that was not benefited, and nearly in the same degree, by a judicious application of pure Bone Dust; and I would here suggest to the advocates of special fertilizers, that in their experiments they try equal weights of pure Bone Dust to the half of the crops of Wheat, Potatoes, Cabbage, or Strawberries, being experimented on by the "specials," and note the results. I do not mean to be understood that these so-called special fertilizers do not answer the purpose of the crop to which they are applied; but what I protest against is, the hair-splitting distinctions claimed for them, confusing and troublesome to the cultivator, if of no practical value.

American commercial florists have, for the past quarter of a century, utterly discarded the various formulas for the preparation of different soils, for the various families of plants cultivated, so dogmatically insisted upon even yet by most European gardeners, and instead of a dozen different mould heaps, usually only one is used, composed of three parts rotted sods and one of rotted stable manure; yet who will say that our results have not been as good in consequence? I believe the same fate is soon to overtake the "specials" in fertilizers. They may hold their own, perhaps, for a time among a few amateur cultivators of 7×9 garden patches, (men usually glib with the pen, and who get in an ecstasy over their success with a dozen Tomato or a score of Strawberry plants,) but few of the hard-fisted gardeners or farmers, who live by the soil, are likely to become converts. My business, as a seedsman, brings me in contact with many hundreds of farmers and gardeners each season, but I have known of few who think it necessary to use special fertilizers for special crops.

It would certainly be a misfortune for the Orange grower of Florida, the Cotton planter of Louisiana, or the Wheat grower of Ohio, if he were induced to freight a special manure for his particular crop a thousand miles, if he had as good a material in Bone Dust at his door. If our law-makers at Washington had given that attention to agriculture that its importance deserves, we would long ago have had suitable grounds there to test such questions on a scale large enough and broad enough to determine whether or not the manure suitable for a Potato was not equally suitable for a Cabbage.

I beg to apologize for the time occupied in discussing fertilizers, but the subject is one of the first importance to every cultivator of the soil, be he farmer, market gardener, nurseryman, or florist; and whether right or wrong in my conclusions, if what has been said may cause further investigation to get at the facts, I shall be satisfied, whatever these facts may reveal.

THE USE OF THE FEET

IN

SOWING AND PLANTING.

BY PETER HENDERSON.

(Read before the annual meeting of the National Association of Nurserymen, Florists, and Seedsmen, held at Cleveland, Ohio, in June, 1880.)

It may be useless to throw out any suggestions in relation to horticultural operations to such a body of practical men as is now before me. Yet I candidly admit that, although I have been extensively engaged in gardening operations for over a quarter of a century, I did not fully realize, until a few years ago, the full importance of how indispensable it is to use the feet in the operations of sowing and planting.

For some years past I have, in writing on gardening matters, insisted upon the great importance of "firming" the soil over the seeds after sowing, especially when the soil is dry, or likely to become so. I know of no operation of more importance in either the farm or the garden, and I trust that what I am about to say will be read and remembered by every one not yet aware of the vast importance of the practice. I say "vast importance," for the loss to the agricultural and horticultural community, from the habit of loosely sowing seeds or planting plants in hot and dry soils, is of a magnitude which few will believe until they have witnessed it ; and it is a loss all the more to be regretted, when we know that by "firming" the soil around the seed or plant, there is, in most cases, a certain preventive.

Particularly in the sowing of seeds, I consider the matter of such vast importance, that it cannot be too often or too strongly told; for the loss to the agricultural and horticultural community, by the neglect of the simple operation of firming the soil around the seed, must amount to many millions annually. For the mischief done is not confined only to the less important garden operations, but even Corn, Cotton, Wheat, Turnips, Grasses, and other important crops of the farm often fail, as thousands of farmers know to their sorrow, in hot and dry soils, by being sown without being firmed sufficiently to prevent the dry air shriveling or drying the seeds. Of course, the use of the feet is impracticable in firming seeds on the farm, but a heavy roller, applied after sowing, is an absolute necessity under certain conditions of the soil, to insure perfect germination, which is indispensable to a perfect crop.

From the middle of April to nearly the end of May of this year, in many sections of the country, there was little or no rain. Such was particularly the case in the vicinity of New York City, where we have hundreds of market gardeners, who cultivate thousands of acres of Cabbage, Cauliflower, and Celery, but the "dry spring" has played sad havoc with their seed-beds. Celery is not one-fourth of a crop, and Cabbage and Cauliflower hardly half, and this failure is due to no other cause than that they persist in sowing their seeds without ever taking the precaution to firm the soil by rolling.

We sow annually about four acres in Celery, Cabbage, and Cauliflower seeds, which produce probably five millions of plants, which we never fail to sell mostly in our immediate neighborhood, to the market gardeners, who have, many of them, even better soil than we have for raising these plants, and would succeed if they would only do as we do, firm the seed after sowing, which is done thus :

After plowing, harrowing, and leveling the land smoothly, lines are drawn by the " marker," which makes furrows about two inches deep and a foot apart. After the man who sows the seed follows another, who, with the ball of the right foot, presses down his full weight on every inch of soil in the drill where the seed has been sown. The rows are then lightly leveled longitudinally with the rake, a light roller is passed over them, and the operation is done.

By this method our crop has never once failed, and what is true of Celery and Cabbage seed is nearly true of all other seeds requiring to be sown during the late spring or summer months.

On July 2d of 1874, as an experiment, I sowed twelve rows of Sweet Corn and twelve rows of Beets, treading in, after sowing, every alternate row of each. In both cases, those trod in came up in four days, while those unfirmed remained twelve days before starting, and would not then have germinated had not rain fallen, for the soil was dry as dust when the seed were sown.

The result was, that the seeds that had been trodden in grew freely from the start, and matured their crops to a marketable condition by fall ; while the rows unfirmed did not mature, as they were not only eight days later in germinating, but the plants were also, to some extent, enfeebled by being partially dried in the loose, dry soil.

This experiment was a most useful one, for it proved that a Corn crop, sown in the vicinity of New York as late as July 2d, could be made to produce "roasting ears" in October, when they never fail to sell freely at high rates ; but the crop would not mature unless the seed germinated at once, which would never be certain at that dry and hot season, unless by this method.

The same season, in August, I treated seeds of Turnips and Spinach in the same way. Those trod in germinated at once, and made an excellent crop, while those unfirmed germinated feebly, and were eventually nearly all burned out by a continuance of dry, hot air penetrating through the loose soil to the tender rootlets.

I beg to caution the inexperienced, however, by no means to tread or roll in seed if the ground is *not dry*. The soil may often be in a suitable condition to sow, and yet be too damp to be trodden upon or rolled. In such cases these operations may not be necessary at all, for if rainy weather ensue, the seeds will germinate of course ; but if there is any likelihood of a continued drought, the treading or rolling may be done a week or more after the seed has been sown, if there is any reason to believe that it may suffer from the dry, hot air. Another very important advantage gained by treading in the seeds is, that when we have crops of Beets, Celery, Turnips, Spinach, or anything else that is sown in rows, the seeds to form the crop come up at once ; while the seeds of the weeds, that are just as liable to perish by the heat as are those of the crop, are retarded. Such of the weed seeds as lie in the space between the rows when the soil is loose, will not germinate as quickly as those of the crop sown ; and hence we can cultivate between the rows before the weeds germinate at all.

Now, if firming the soil around seed, to protect it from the influence of a dry and hot atmosphere, is a necessity, it is obvious that it is quite as much so in the case of plants, whose rootlets are even more sensitive to such influence than the dormant seed.

Experienced professional horticulturists, however, are less likely to neglect this than to neglect in the case of seeds, for the damage from such neglect is easier to be seen, and hence better understood by the practical nurseryman; but with the inexperienced amateur the case is different. When he receives his package of trees or plants from the nurseryman, he handles them as if they were glass, every broken twig or root calls forth a complaint, and he proceeds to plant them, gingerly straightening out each root and sifting the soil around them, but he would no more stamp down that soil than he would stamp on the soil of his mother's grave. So the plant, in nine cases out of ten, is left loose and waggling; the dry air penetrates through the soil to its roots; the winds shake it; it shrivels up and fails to grow; and then come the anathemas on the head of the unfortunate nurseryman, who is charged with selling him dead trees or plants.

About a month ago I sent a package of a dozen Roses by mail to a lady in Savannah. She wrote me a woeful story last week, saying that, though the Roses had arrived seemingly all right, they had all died but one, and what was very singular, she said, the one that lived was the one that Mr. Jones had stepped on, and which she had thought sure was crushed to death, for Mr. Jones weighs 200 pounds. Now, though I do not advise any gentleman of 200 pounds putting his brogan on the top of a tender Rose plant, as a practice conducive to its health, yet, if Mrs. Jones could have allowed her weighty lord to press the soil against the root of each of her dozen Roses, I much doubt if she would now have to mourn their loss.

It has often been a wonder to many of us, who have

been workers in the soil for a generation, how some of the simplest methods of culture have not been practised until we were nearly done with life's work.

There are few of us but have had such experience, personally, I must say that I never pass through a year but I am confounded to find that some operation can not only be quicker done, but better done than we have been in the habit of doing it.

These improvements loom up from various causes, but mainly from suggestions thrown out by our employees in charge of special departments, a system which we do all in our power to encourage.

As a proof of the value of such improvements, which have led to simplifying our operations, I will state the fact, that though our area of green-house surface is now more than double that which it was in 1870, and the land used in our florist's business one third more, yet the number of hands employed is less now than in 1870, and yet, at the same time, the quality of our stock is infinitely better now than then.

Whether it is the higher price of labor in this country that forces us into labor-saving expedients, or the interchange of opinions from the greater number of nationalities centering here, that gives us broader views of culture, I am not prepared to state; but that America is now selling nearly all the products of the green-house, garden, nursery, and farm, lower than is done in Europe, admits of no question; and if my homely suggestions in this matter of firming the soil around newly planted seeds or plants, will in any degree assist us in still holding to the front, I shall be gratified.

I have now been a writer for the horticultural press for over thirty years, and am egotistical enough to believe that many of my suggestions, born of a lifetime of active practical work in all kinds of gardening operations, have benefited hundreds; but I consider the short paper here given on "The Use of the Feet in Sowing and Planting" the most important and valuable I have ever written, if I have succeeded in making my meaning clear; for the ignorance on this subject is widespread; and when we consider the hundreds of thousands of acres of all kinds of farm products that fail annually from no other cause than that the seeds have not been properly firmed in the soil, we can readily imagine the loss from such neglect and the importance of making known the remedy.

Although, to the thousands of amateurs who are interested in gardening work, the loss resulting from a few seeds failing to germinate, or a few newly-planted plants failing to grow, is not often estimated by dollars and cents, yet the annoyance and disappointment of failure are inducements enough to use the best means to attain success, which I believe will rarely fail to be attained if the directions which have been given for "The Use of the Feet in Sowing and Planting" be strictly followed; for the necessity for the operation of firming the soil is just as essential in the tiniest flower bed of the garden as in the large plots of the market garden or the broad acres of the farm.

The above essay on "The Use of the Feet in Sowing and Planting" was delivered at the annual meeting of the National Association of Nurserymen, Florists, and Seedsmen, held in Cleveland, Ohio, in 1880, and at the meeting held in Chicago the next season I was gratified by the information obtained from a gentleman connected with the press, who publicly stated that the above article had been copied and republished in hundreds of newspapers throughout the land, and that the information it contained had, no doubt, already been worth hundreds of thousands of dollars to the community. Believing this statement to be true is a sufficient excuse for again reproducing it in its present form in "Garden and Farm Topics," as in this way we bring it permanently before the hosts of new readers annually springing up.

POPULAR ERRORS
AND
SCIENTIFIC DOGMAS IN HORTICULTURE.

BY PETER HENDERSON.

(Read before the New York Horticultural Society in 1881.)

IN nearly all matters of life, before accepting some one's say so, it is wisdom first to use our own judgment and common sense ; and this is particularly true in many of the operations of horticulture, for in no profession is there greater need for the reasoning faculties, and in the neglect of the use of these, the most absurd errors and delusions are held even by many who are practically engaged in the business. The breeder of fancy fowls or pigeons could not be told that the plumage of either would ever assume the scarlet of the Flamingo, though he would likely be quite ready to believe that his next-door neighbor, who is a flower fancier, may yet have a blue Rose or a blue Dahlia, phenomena just as unlikely as that his Dorkings or his Brahmas would have a plumage of scarlet ; for, so far, we find that there is no such thing in nature as plants having scarlet, yellow, and blue flowers, in varieties of the same species. Perhaps the nearest approach to it is in the Hyacinth ; but in it, although we have yellow and blue, we have no true scarlet.

Another very popular error is the belief that something mysterious is done by the professional horticulturist to produce new or fine varieties of fruits or flowers.

There is no mystery or skill about it, other than to select the best or fittest and place them together. This done, man's work is done: Nature does the rest. It is laid down almost as an axiom, by amateur horticulturists, that the water with which plants are watered should be soft or rain water, and of the temperature of the room or green-house wherein the plants are. Commercial florists, who grow hundreds of thousands of plants, cannot do this; and yet, as a rule, their plants are in the very best possible health, far better than that of the amateur who goes to this unnecessary trouble, for the reason that the real conditions of success (the proper temperature or moisture) can be given in the green-house, but not in ordinary sitting-rooms.

Then, too, the flower-loving amateur is trammeled by another dogma, this time bearing the authority of quasi-science; for a great man, the family doctor, armed with a smattering of chemical lore, glibly asserts that plants, at night, give out carbonic acid gas, which is poisonous to animal life, and, consequently, if plants are kept in sleeping-rooms, sickness and even death may follow. No theory can be more destitute of truth. That plants give out carbonic acid gas at night may be, but that it is in quantity enough to endanger human life is utter nonsense. If it were so, we would have no insects attacking plants, for their low organization would make them the first victims to a gas as poisonous as carbonic acid. Besides, most gardeners who have had charge of green-house plants, know that on cold nights the most comfortable quarter is the green-house ; and yet I think it would be difficult to find in any business a healthier class of men than professional gardeners. I have pleasure in believing that my denunciations of this absurdity, begun over twenty years ago, has had something to do in checking its spread; but thousands of plants, particularly in the rural districts, are yet consigned to the coal cellar, at the dictum of some wiseacre of a village doctor, who is happy to be thought thus learned in the chemistry of plants.

It is a common error to expect, in any one greenhouse, conservatory, or other place where plants are kept, that a general variety can be grown and do well. If you attempt to grow Carnations or Roses in the same temperature in which Coleus, Poinsettias, or Bouvardias will thrive, rest assured they will complain of too much heat; while, on the other hand, if you treat these plants of the tropics to the atmosphere suited to the health of a Carnation or a Rose, they will soon show evidence of starvation, so that when any housewife attempts to keep plants of such widely different latitudes in her sitting-room, she must not be surprised if the results with all are not satisfactory. So, too, gentlemen employing gardeners, who have only one temperature to operate in, will be unjust and unreasonable to expect satisfactory results if plants from temperate and tropical countries are obliged to be grown together.

Another widespread delusion, of a very different kind, pervades a large class of men, who have a taste for horticultural matters, but who have no practical knowledge of the business. They have land lying idle adjacent to a town or city; they see growers of fruit, flowers, or vegetables alongside of them, rough, unlettered fellows, perhaps, making the business a success; why should they, with their lands, not do likewise? They hire a manager, and plunge into the business of market gardener or florist, and in nineteen cases out of twenty lose all they invest. Nothing else need be expected. What chance would a blacksmith have if he hired a dry-goods or a grocery clerk to run either of these businesses, if he were ignorant himself of the grocery or dry-goods trade? There is no more true adage, applied to horticulture as a business, than that

> "He who by the plow would thrive,
> Himself must either hold or drive;"

for he who attempts any branch of it, dependent upon the knowledge of others, without taking a hold himself to attain that knowledge, is almost certain to come to grief.

A class of scientific men, at the present time, are greatly exercising the minds of a large portion of the professional farmers and gardeners, as well as amateurs, in the matter of fertilizers. These gentlemen have discovered that certain kinds of plants have their structure composed of different elements, and their aim is to put in the soil the elements that are found in the several families of plants. Some dealers in fertilizers advertise not less than thirty different kinds, which they claim are specially adapted for so many kinds of plants. Thus, the Orange grower of Florida is told that a special manure is to be found in the "Orange Fertilizers," manufactured in New York or Philadelphia, and, if he has faith in the claim, is induced to freight a material which is no better, for the purpose wanted, than what may be bought at less cost at his door. So, too, the Tobacco grower of Kentucky, the Potato grower of New York, or the Wheat growers of far-off Minnesota or California, are told by so-called science that there are fertilizers specially adapted for these crops. I do not for a moment dispute that the special fertilizers claimed for special crops do not answer for these crops; but that these specialties are a necessity is the point questioned. There are few practical agriculturists but believe that, if all the thirty specialties were mixed together and applied to the special crops, the result would be equally as good as if the hair-splitting distinction of a separate fertilizer for each crop was used. Some chemists tell us that phosphorus enters largely into the human brain, and that a fish diet is necessary for the best development of brains. Broad results are the best test of the dogmas of so-called science ; and it scarcely can be shown that fish-eating nations or communities are specially noted for extraordinary brain development.

Charles Darwin has said, and he finds many believers, that certain plants, such as the *Drosera* or Sundew, and our own Carolina Fly-trap, (*Dionæa muscipula,*) are fed by the insects that their wonderful structure enables them to catch. In conjunction with a friend, a few years ago, I made most extensive and careful experiments in our green-houses, covering a period of six months, with several hundred plants of the Carolina Fly-trap, and the result showed that of two lots, treated exactly in the same manner, those fed with insects in no way differed from those that were not so fed, which satisfied me that, if the plants digested the insects placed in the leaf trap, the food was in no way beneficial.

While these experiments were going on, they were watched with great interest by hundreds, and nearly all were convinced that the belief that any plants feed on insects is a delusion, although Mr. Darwin has written a book of 400 pages in the attempt to prove it a fact. Still, it may be presumption to question such an authority; and, as I had no other object in my experiments but to get at the facts, I will be pleased, at any time, to furnish any member of our Society enough plants of the Fly-trap to experiment with, free of cost, so that this question may be more definitely settled.

For hundreds of years the art of grafting and budding has been practised, the object being to perpetuate varieties that could not well be increased by cuttings or layers ; and it had been almost universally believed, until a few years ago, by nurserymen and gardeners, that the stock in no manner affected the individuality of the variety budded or grafted upon it, except to make it stronger or weaker, according to the nature of the stock budded or grafted upon.

But when Mr. Darwin, in 1868, issued his famous work on "Animals and Plants under Domestication," he started the theory of what is called "graft hybrids," and gave a number of instances, where seemingly there was amalgamation of the stock and graft. The most important case instanced is where a Mr. Adam inserted a bud of Cytisus purpureus into the Cytisus Laburnum, and the result was that the bud, when it developed, had yellow and purple racemes on different shoots ; on others the purple and yellow were intermingled on the same raceme, and seemingly partook of the nature of both varieties. Another case is instanced of the Bizzaria Orange, which originated two hundred and fifty years ago in France, on which Oranges and Citrons are found on the same tree, distinct, and in some fruits blended.

Again, he cites various instances where the bud or graft of a variegated plant has the effect of causing variegation in the green-leaved stock. Nearly every gardener is familiar with this. If he takes a green-leaved, white-flowered Abutilon and grafts the Abutilon Thompsonii on it, with its variegated leaves and orange flowers, the variegation will affect the leaves of the white variety, but no other change occurs ; the flowers hold their own shape and color, and in no respect are they changed. A variegated single white-flowered Oleander grafted on a plain-leaved red variety will, as in the Abutilon, blotch the leaves, but will in no way change the color or condition of the double red flower. So in the case of Buist's variegated red Althea, when grafted on a double white; it in no other way affects the color or doubleness of the flower, but it again blotches the leaves white with the disease, variegation. I consider it was most unfortunate for Mr. Darwin to have advanced the peculiarity of variegated leaves as bearing on his theory of "graft hybrids," for almost in every instance where a variegated variety is grafted on a plain green-leaved stock, it taints the healthy plant with variegation, though it changes it in no other respect; just as a small-pox victim may be marked with that disease, but in no other way changed.

Negative evidence is not usually good evidence, but when we know that countless millions of fruits and flowers have, in the past one hundred years, been budded and grafted without the individuality of the variety being in any way affected by the stock, and that only a few instances, such as the Cytisus purpureus and the Bizzaria Orange, can be cited as exceptions, is it not fair to infer that these almost solitary cases are due to what Mr. Darwin calls "Bud Variation?" a condition by no means uncommon in scores of families of plants which are never budded or grafted. Nearly all of us see every season scarlet, and scarlet and white striped Carnations on the same plant. Dahlias are found crimson, crimson and white, and sometimes almost white on the same plant. Last spring we had plants of the double scarlet Hibiscus, with scarlet, orange, and scarlet and orange—three distinct kinds of flowers on the same plant; and that wonderful freak of nature, the striped Tea Rose, American Banner, was a "sport" from a plant of Bon

Silene, and has no resemblance to it, either in flower or foliage.

Scores of other instances could be cited, if time would permit; but enough has been shown, I think, at least to throw doubt on the theory, that the stock affects the individuality of the graft. In the past quarter of a century, millions upon millions of Bartlett Pears and Baldwin Apples have been grafted upon millions of stocks; and yet to-day they are as true to their individuality as the Concord Grape or Wilson's Strawberry, that are perpetuated by cuttings or runners, and not one of them is in any way changed from what it was when it first appeared, unless by the temporary accidents of soil or climate.

I believe that the smallest or the greatest of God's creations has a separate and distinct individuality, and that they cannot be blended, except by generation, and that the product of generation, whether in the lowest microscopic germ, or in the highest type, man, has an individuality distinct and separate that it cannot attach to another.

HUMBUGS IN HORTICULTURE.

BY PETER HENDERSON.

(An Essay Read at the Annual Meeting of the National Association of Nurserymen, Florists, and Seedsmen, held at Chicago., Ill., June 16, 1880.)

THE life-time experience of any man is not too short to be imposed upon by many of the hundreds of old varieties of fruits, flowers, or vegetables that are sent out annually under new names. Any well-posted nurseryman can easily detect when a Bartlett Pear or a Baldwin Apple appears under a new name; or a florist, making a specialty of Roses, knows, as, for example, when, some years ago, the old Solfaterre Rose was sent out under the name of "Augusta," (claiming it to be hardy in every State of the Union, and sold as a great bargain at $5 apiece,) that the venders thereof were either swindlers or entirely ignorant of the business they had embarked in; or when the confiding market gardener is induced to buy a new and superior Cabbage or Tomato seed at $5 an ounce, and finds them identical with varieties that he can buy at half that price per pound, he has good reason to come to the conclusion that the man from whom he purchased was either a humbug or else unfitted, from his ignorance, to engage in the business of a seedsman.

But, unfortunately, from the varied nature of these impostures, it is exceedingly difficult to mete out justice to those who, knowingly or otherwise, place such swindles on the horticultural community; for the man who grows fruit trees is as likely to know as little about Roses as the man who grows Roses is to know about fruit trees, and either is less likely to be posted on the merits of vegetables. So, then, if the partly experienced horticulturist may be imposed upon in such a way, how safe is the field when the swindler tries his tricks on the general public.

The sharp man of the city falls as quickly into the trap of the horticultural swindler as the veriest rustic, because his city experience of impostures in other matters helps him nothing in this. He may not be much troubled when he sees a bootblack fall off the dock into the river, particularly if his companion plays off the heroic *role*, and plunges in after him to the rescue. He understands it all, for both can swim like ducks, and there was no more danger for the first than for the second, and none for either. A well-stuffed pocket-book snatched from under his feet is an incident that does not in the least arouse his cupidity, for he has long been conversant with the trick of the pocket-book dropper. The mock auctioneer may scream himself hoarse, offering gold watches at $5 apiece, and it hardly elicits a smile of derision. The tears of the benighted orphan in search of his uncle does not bring a dime from his pocket, for he understands it all, together with a score more of the tricks of the great city. But in the springtime, when his garden instincts begin to bud, and he sees in some window in Broadway flaming representations of fruits and flowers, he falls into the trap and is ready for the spoiler.

Some years ago I had occasion to act as an amateur detective in one of these horticultural swindling shops, the owners of which are now known in New York as the "Blue Rose Men." When I arrived, there were at least a dozen ladies and gentlemen engaged in buying seeds, bulbs, and plants, the flowers and fruits of which were represented by the pictures on the walls: for example, Asparagus was shown as having shoots as thick as a broom handle, the seeds of which were selling rapidly at one cent apiece, warranted to produce a crop in three months from the time of sowing; an old lady had just become the possessor of $5 worth, and seemed delighted with her bargain.

One of the most attractive pictures on the wall was an immense colored engraving, showing a tree, on which Strawberries were growing, and as big as Oranges. My gaze was attracted to a handsome plate of Blue Moss Roses, and I modestly asked the price of the plants. The polite Frenchman (who was doing the principal selling for the concern) whisked out from beneath the table three plants, representing them to be Moss Roses, (which, by-the-way, were all alike, and were all our common Prairie Rose,) and said, "This one, he bloom only once, I tell you the truth, so I sell him for two dollar. This one, he be the Remontant, he bloom twice—just twice— I sell him for three dollar; but this one, he be the ever-blooming, perpetual Blue Moss Rose, he bloom all the time, he cheap at $5." I quietly remarked, if it bloomed all the time, why was it not blooming now? He looked at me pityingly, and said, "My dear sir, you expect too much. These Moss Rose just come over in the ship from Paris. You take him home and plant him, and he bloom right away, and he keep on blooming." I did not take him home, but I took the story, something in the shape it is now told, and had it published in one of the leading New York papers, and in less than a week the "Blue Rose Men" had pulled up stakes, but, no doubt, to pitch their camp somewhere else, and set their traps for fresh victims. The "Blue Rose Men" are very impartial in their wanderings, and rarely omit a city of any size, beginning usually in New Orleans in January, rounding northward, and ending up with Philadelphia, New York, and Boston through April and May.

These humbugs in horticulture have their comical side. The other year, in passing St. Paul's Church, (Broadway,) New York, I saw an old negro squatted on the pavement with a great bundle of plants, carefully mossed up, lying alongside of him. On inquiring what they were, he said they were Rose bushes; Rose bushes having all the attributes wanted in a Rose, fragrance, hardiness, and everblooming, and the price but fifty cents apiece. He had got them, he said, from the boss, and was selling them on a commission. The poor darkey was only an innocent agent. He no doubt believed he was selling Rose bushes, but the boss, whoever he might be, undoubtedly knew better, for the plants were not Roses at all, but the common Cat Brier, (*Smilax sarsaparilla,*) one of the worst pests of our hedgerows, but the plant of which is near enough in appearance to a Rose to deceive the ordinary city merchant.

That same season at every prominent street corner could be seen the venders of the "Alligator Plant," which some enterprising genius had cut by the wagon load from the Jersey swamps, and dealt them out to those who retailed them on the street.

The "Alligator Plant" was sold in lengths of twelve to twenty inches, at from twenty-five to fifty cents apiece, according to its straightness and length; and by the number engaged in the business, hundreds of dollars' worth must have been sold. The "Alligator Plant" is the rough, triangular branches of the Sweet Gum Tree, (*Liquidambar styraciflua,*) common in most parts of the country. There is no doubt whatever that these pieces of stick have been planted by thousands during the last two years in the gardens in and around New York, with about as much chance of their growing as the fence pickets.

The bulb peddlers, a class of itinerant swindlers, deserve brief attention. They have always some wonderful novelty in bulbs; and their mode of operating, to the uninitiated, has a semblance of fairness, as they are liberal fellows, and frankly offer to take one-half cash on delivery, and if the goods do not come up to the representation, the other half need not be paid. For example, when the Gold-banded Japan Lily was first introduced, bulbs the size of hickory nuts sold at $250 per hundred. About that time one of these worthies came along with samples of a Lily of fine size and appearance, with which, he said, he had just arrived from Japan. There was no doubt of its genuineness, for he had seen it in flower. He had a large stock, and would sell at $100 per hundred, but he was willing to take half that amount down, and the other half when it flowered and had proved correct. It did not prove correct, and he never called. The bulb he sold was the common White Lily, (*Lilium candidum,*) which is sold everywhere at $5 or $6 per hundred. These same scamps flood the rural districts every year with blue Gladiolus, scarlet Tuberoses, and other absurdities in bulbs and seeds, usually on the same terms of one-half cash down, the other half when the *rara avis* has feathered out. It is needless to say that they never try it twice on the same victim, but avail themselves of our broad continent to seek out new fields for their operations.

One of the most successful swindlers of this type was Comanche George, whose fame became national. George made his advent in New York in 1876. He was, he said, a Texas scout, and for years his rifle, revolver, and bowie knife had been the terror of the red men; but one day, in his rambles on the lone Texas prairies, his eye was arrested by a flower, whose wonderful coloring eclipsed the rainbow, and whose delicate perfume was wafted over the Brazos for leagues; in short, never before had eye of mortal rested on such a flower. The man of war was subdued. He betook himself to the peaceful task of gathering seed, and turned his steps to the haunts of civilized man to distribute it.

We first heard of him in Washington, where he wished to place it in the hands of the government, and accordingly offered it to Mr. William Smith, Superintendent of the Botanic Gardens there; but the government, so Smith said, was not just then in a position to buy, and with his advice George trimmed his sails for New York and a market. His success in Baltimore and Philadelphia was so great (where he started the sale of the seeds at two cents apiece) that it induced him, when he struck New York, to advance the price to five cents a seed. He put up at one of the best hotels, and claimed that for a month his sales of the seed of the Cockatelle—the beautiful Texas flower—reached $50 a day. But his success threw him off his balance; he took to fire water, and in an unguarded moment fell into the hands of a newspaper man, who extracted from him all the facts connected with the enterprise. George never was a scout, had never been in Texas, but he had been a good customer to the various seedsmen of the different cities, where his purchases of Okra or Gumbo seed, at about fifty cents a pound, had made nearly a dearth of the article. His victims (whose names he gave by the score, and which were duly chronicled in the newspaper article referred to) were from all classes: the enterprising florist, who secretly went into it in a wholesale way, with a view to outwit his less fortunate fellows; the grandee of Fifth Avenue, who anticipated a blaze of beauty on his lawn; the hotel man, whose window boxes were to perfume the air; all had fallen easy victims to the wiles of Comanche George. George disappeared from New York, though there is but little doubt that his business had been too successful for him to abandon it. A newspaper paragraph, cut from a paper last week, which reads as follows, looks as if it might be the Texas scout in a somewhat different *role:*

"The prepossessing appearance, gentlemanly demeanor, and foreign accent of the man who called himself Carlo Corella, botanist to the Court of Brazil, convinced a number of wealthy San Francisco ladies that he was truthful. He said to each that the failure of a remittance compelled him to sell some rare bulbs of Brazilian Lilies, which he had intended to present to Mrs. R. B. Hayes. 'The flower,' says the *Chronicle*, 'was to be a great scarlet bell, with ecru ruchings on the petals, a solferino frill around the pistil, and a whole bottle of perfumery in each stamen.' He sold about fifty almost worthless bulbs at $4 each."

The nurserymen present are no doubt better posted in the swindles practised in their particular department than I am; but operators engage in different lines in different parts of the country: for example, we have never yet seen in the Eastern States any one trying to sell an apple tree bearing blue apples as big as melons, as we were told, at our meeting at Cleveland last year, had been successfully done in Ohio and Illinois. Still we have men of fair ability in the nursery swindling line, one of whom last winter succeeded in disposing of hundreds of winter-bearing grapes, by carrying with him a few good bunches of the white Malaga of the shops.

One great detriment, not only to the florist, but to the purchaser, is begotten of these swindles in horticulture.

The purchaser of flowers in our markets must have his plants in bloom, because he has been at times so swindled that he must now see what he buys. In New York, the amateur rarely buys from the grower, but from the agent or middleman who sells in the market stands or street corners. These, whether men or women, are generally entirely ignorant of the nature of plants, and most of them have no responsibility, and they rarely fail to make their wares accord with the wants of the purchaser: nearly every plant is hardy, ever-blooming, and has all the qualities desired by the buyer.

But now and then these swindles become a serious matter to the victim. Some years ago a typical Englishman, who had been a green grocer in Covent Garden Market, London, found his way to New York. He at once discovered an almost entire absence of Cauliflowers in our markets, and what few there were, were sold at prices four times those of London. He soon made up his mind to make his fortune, and, at the same time, show the Yankees something they did not know. He duly selected and prepared the ground for an acre, and one day in May he sallied into the market to procure his Cauliflower plants. This he found no difficulty in doing, for at Dutch Peggy's (in those days the headquarters for all kinds of herbs, plants, and seeds) they were to be seen by the wagon load. Ten thousand were procured, the quantity for his acre, and, duly planted, they began to grow apace. He had planted the 1st of May. If it had been in England, his Cauliflower heads would have been ready about the 1st of July, but something was evidently wrong in the Yankee climate. His Cauliflowers grew through June, through July into August, only to develop into fine specimens of Drumhead Cabbage, then of hardly the value he had paid for them as

Cauliflower plants. He got out of the business thoroughly disgusted; and in telling his sorrowful tale to me a year afterward, he related that when he went to expostulate with old Peggy about having blasted his prospects, before he could get a word said, she recognized him as a customer, and demanded to know if he did not again want some more early Cauliflower plants.

I have said old Peggy was also a vender of seeds. It is now something over thirty years ago that a young florist presented himself before her and purchased an ounce of Mignonette. Ever alive to business, Peggy asked him if he had tried the new red Mignonette. He protested there was no such thing, but Peggy's candid manner persuaded him, and fifty cents were invested. The seed looked familiar, and when it sprouted it looked more familiar; when it bloomed it was far too familiar, for it was Red Clover. Peggy has long since been gathered to her fathers, and I have entirely forgiven her for selling me the red Mignonette.

Perhaps there is no swindling that is more extensively practised, and which so cruelly injures the operators of the soil, as that of adulteration in fertilizers. The great mass of our farmers and gardeners are poor men, who can ill afford even to pay for the pure fertilizers necessary to grow their crops, and to pay money and high freights on adulterations worse than useless, is hard indeed. The ignorance of those dealing in such wares does much to spread the evil. A fellow came into my office last summer with samples of a fertilizer, nicely put up in cans, which he claimed could be sold in immense quantities by the seedsmen, as it had not only the wonderful properties of invigorating and stimulating all planted crops, but that it at the same time would kill all noxious weeds. I need not say that he had waked up the wrong passenger, and that he made a rapid movement toward the door. Yet, notwithstanding the impudence and absurdity of such a claim, the scamp was enabled to prowl around the vicinity of New York for weeks, and, undoubtedly, sold to hundreds. If he had said he had a cannon from which, when grape shot was fired into a crowd, it killed only enemies—never friends—the one claim would have been as reasonable as the other.

There is another species of humbugging, which, though it can hardly be called swindling, is somewhat akin to it. I refer to the men who claim to have secrets by which they can accomplish extraordinary results in the propagation and culture of plants. I can well remember, in my early days, that the nursery propagator was looked upon as a sort of demi-god, possessing secrets known only to himself and a favored few, whose interest it was to continue to throw dust in the eyes of every young aspirant after knowledge. The door of the propagating house was locked and bolted, as if it were a Bastile, and even the proprietor (if he were unfortunate enough not to have practical knowledge) was allowed entrance only as a special favor; for his propagator was an autocrat, of whom he stood in awe and reverence. But since the advent of horticultural publications in America, particularly during the past fifteen or twenty years, the "secrets" of these pretentious fellows have had such ventilation, that now nearly every operation of the green-house is as well understood by the tens of thousands engaged in the business, as the operation of the farm is by the farmer.

The most of these pretenders to this secret knowledge of horticulture are foreigners, though occasionally a native tries it on. Some fifteen years ago, when the grape-vine mania was at its height, an old Connecticut Yankee pretended he had discovered a new method of propagating the grape, which he would impart for a consideration to the highest bidder. He issued a profusion of hand bills to the trade, asking for bids, modestly requesting the receiver of the hand bill to hang it up in a conspicuous place.

I sent my copy to my friend Meehan, of the *Gardener's Monthly*, saying that the pages of that magazine were the most conspicuous place I knew of to comply with the wish of the old gentleman. Mr. Meehan not only inserted the advertisement gratis, and in the most conspicuous manner, but he did more, for he appended below the advertisement a few remarks I had ventured to make on the subject. This opened the ball, and for six months the pages of the *Gardener's Monthly* became the battle ground for the opinions of the discoverer and myself. But the gratuitous advertisement did not avail him much, for he and his secret soon passed into oblivion, and was heard from no more. There are no secrets in horticulture. The laws that govern the germination of a seed, the rooting of a cutting, or the taking of a bud or graft, are the same now as they were a thousand years ago, and anyone pretending to have any secret knowledge in the matter is either an ignoramus or an impostor.

Since the above was written several other swindling schemes have been perpetrated. Among others, the bulb man has turned up again. Having for the time being become too well known in the city, he has betaken himself to the rural districts, where he plied his trade last fall most successfully, finding his victims chiefly among confiding women. Taking pattern of the "Blue Rose Man," he has provided himself with gaudy pictures of impossible Lilies, which ought to deceive none but the thoughtless or ignorant. As a matter of precaution, it may be well to describe his methods of operating. His first move is to learn the names of the wealthiest and best known people in the neighborhood. He then begins his canvass, calling at houses where he has reason to believe none of the male members of the family are at home. He has just returned from California, where he had the great good fortune to discover three kinds of the most gorgeous of all Lilies, hitherto entirely unknown, and now for the first and only time offered for sale. Their size is immense, the colors gorgeous, and the fragrance lovely. No such Lilies have been seen before. He has sold Mrs. Brown, and Mrs. Smith, and Mrs. Jones (naming well-known neighbors) bulbs of each of the three kinds at four and five dollars a bulb; but as he has only a few left, and is anxious to get home, he will sell the remainder at two and three dollars each. His victims hesitate in doubt a few moments, and then drop into the net. I had the pleasure of blocking this fellow's game in one instance, appearing on the scene just in time to do so. In one locality, within my personal knowledge, this man sold dozens of these bulbs to confiding victims. I saw some of these "gorgeous" new California Lilies when they came into flower, and they were all neither more nor less than the common white garden Lily, (*Lilium candidum,*) fine bulbs of which can always be bought for twenty cents or less.

Another instance may be mentioned, in which the rogue offered for sale, at a dollar a paper, the seed of a variety of Mignonette, even more famous than the red Mignonette of Aunt Peggy, mentioned above. This bore magnificent spikes of flowers, nearly two feet long and of delicious fragrance.

A lady friend, one of his victims, carefully sowed the seeds, and waited anxiously for the appearance of the plants. The seedlings proved to be so vigorous that she ventured to separate and transplant them in the open border. They grew and grew till they finally rivaled in growth the famous mustard seed mentioned in the good Book. The reader will probably smile when I tell him that this famous Mignonette proved to be Pearl Millet.

The following from the New York *Tribune* of February 19th, 1882, shows that occasionally these enterprising gentlemen receive their deserts:

"The case of John Harrison, the industrious seed peddler, who was locked up in Newark the other day, is one which calls for commiseration. It was a propitious season for business in his line, for the near approach of spring had begun to warm up the desire to worry the soil and plant something, a desire that slumbers in the bosom of every man or woman who is the proprietor of a garden, a back yard, or even of a flower pot. Our vender was therefore driving a brisk trade, when he was arrested for obtaining money under false pretenses. The pretense and falsehood charged were Mr. Harrison's statement that his seeds, when dropped into water or earth, would speedily germinate and grow into a bush, which would suddenly burst into beautiful and fragrant bloom, and then bear a rich fruitage of 'wash-rags;' a crop which at once commended itself to the cleanly and thrifty housewives of New Jersey. Now there is a well-known vine of the cucumber family which flourishes in the West Indies, and bears a gourd-like fruit, the spongy lining of whose tough shell is used by the simple islanders to brush their huts with when they have any, and for toilet and culinary cleansing as well. Mr. Harrison's descriptions of this vegetable may have been a trifle too eloquent, but surely a merciful magistrate would consider this nothing more than justifiable professional exaggeration. Any one who has been attacked by a roving tree agent, armed with a book full of colored lithographic plates of trees clad with rainbow-hued foliage, and decorated still further with fruit of marvelous shape and bulk, will understand that Mr. Harrison is not a unique sinner, but simply a man who understands his business."

This list of humbugs on horticultural subjects might be greatly extended, but perhaps enough has been said to put the intelligent and thoughtful reader on his guard in the future.

DRAINING.

THIS is one of the most important operations in horticulture. No matter how fertile the normal condition of the soil; no matter how abundantly it is fertilized; no matter how carefully and thoroughly it is tilled, if water remain in it at the depth at which roots penetrate, all labor will be in vain; for no satisfactory result can ever be attained until the water is drained off. The subject is one of such importance that we cannot give it full attention here, and to such as need to operate on a large scale, works specially devoted to the subject should be consulted, or a draining engineer employed. Soils having a gravelly or sandy sub-soil ten or twenty inches below the top soil do not usually need draining, but in all soils underlaid by clay or hard pan, draining is indispensable, unless in cases where there is a slope of two to three feet in a hundred; and even in such cases draining is beneficial if the sub-soil is clay.

In soils having a clay or hard-pan sub-soil, drains should be made three feet deep, and not more than twenty feet apart. If stones are plenty, they may be profitably used to fill up the drains, say to a depth of twelve or fifteen inches, either placed so as to form a "rubble" drain, if the stones are round, or built with an orifice at the bottom, if the stones are flat. In either case care must be used to cover the stones carefully up with inverted sods, or some material that will prevent the soil being washed through the stones and choking up the drain.

Drain tiles, when they can be obtained at a reasonable price, are the best material for draining. A horseshoe pattern is generally used. If the drain has a hard bottom they can be placed directly on it when leveled to the proper grade; but if the ground is soft and spongy, a board must be laid in the bottom, on which to place the tiles. It is often a very troublesome matter to get the few drain tiles necessary to drain a small garden, and in such cases an excellent and cheap substitute can be had by using one of boards. Take ordinary rough boards, Pine, Hemlock, or Spruce, and cut them into widths of three or four inches, and nail them together so as to form a triangular pipe, taking care to "break the joints" in putting the lengths together. Care must be taken that the boards are not nailed together too closely, else they might swell so as to prevent the water passing into the drain to be carried off. These drains are usually set with a flat side down, but they will keep clear better if put with a point down, though it is more trouble to lay them. Drains made in this way will last twenty years or more.

Of course, in draining, the greater the fall that can be got the better, though, if the grading is carefully done by a competent engineer, a very slight fall will suffice. Some of the trunk or main sewers in our cities have only a grade of one foot in a thousand.

Drainage in flower pots is essential for most plants, whenever the pot is over five inches in diameter. Charcoal broken into pieces from one-half to one inch in diameter I prefer to every other kind of drainage, which should be in depth from one inch to four inches, according to the size of the pot to be drained, an extra quantity being necessary if the plant is being shifted into a pot too large; then ample drainage is indispensable to admit of the quick escape of water. This drainage, so called, is not alone of use as a means for the rapid escape of water, but also for the admission of air to the roots, which brings in another important matter in connection with the drainage in pots, the necessity of standing the pots on some rough material, (when solid benches are used in the green-house, or when placed in the open air in beds,) such as gravel or cinders; for if placed on sand, soil, or anything that will close up the orifice in the bottom of the pot, all the drainage placed in it will avail nothing. It is far better to use no drainage at all, and stand the pots on a rough surface, than to use the drainage and place the plants on some material that will close the outlet. If, however, the bench is formed of slate, or boards that have been cemented over, so as to form a smooth surface, there is no necessity for placing any gravel or other rough material under the pots, as such a surface will allow the water to pass from the pots more freely than if anything, such as gravel, were placed under them. For very large pots slatted benches are best.

Many years ago, in some of my first writings on the subject of drainage in pots, I admit to having taken rather too radical ground against the practice, because, in those days, everybody almost used to "crock" or drain the very smallest pots. The absurdity of this soon became apparent to me, as I found that, with hardly an exception, for plants in pots up to the size of four inches, it was worse than useless to drain; and as all my practice, up to that time, had been with pots but little larger than four inches, I rather rashly jumped to the conclusion that, in our warm, dry atmosphere, the European practice of crocking *all sizes* of flower pots might be wholly dispensed with here; but added experience showed that, even in our dry atmosphere, flower pots of five inches diameter and upward, in which are grown Roses or other plants whose roots are sensitive to moisture, had better be crocked or drained. It is not pleasant to admit an error, particularly when promulgated in print for the "instruction" of others; but it is better to make what amend is possible by making the acknowledgment, than to continue to stick to opinions before given when there is reason to believe these were formed in error.

THE END.

GARDENING FOR PROFIT.
BY
PETER HENDERSON.

To such as are intending to begin the business of Market Gardening, we offer for their instruction our work "Gardening for Profit," published first in 1866, and a new edition in 1873. "Gardening for Profit" has had a larger sale, probably, than any work ever published on the subject of Horticulture. Upward of *fifty thousand* copies have been sold, and we have hundreds of grateful testimonials from those who have been benefited by its teachings. The subjects of its contents are:

The Men fitted for the Business.—Amount of Capital required and Working Force per Acre.—Profits of Market Gardening.—The Market Gardens near London.—Location, Situation, and Laying Out.—Soils, Drainage, and Preparation.—Manures.—Implements.—The Uses and Management of Cold Frames.—The Formation and Management of Hot-beds.—Forcing Pits and Green-houses.—Seeds and Seed Raising.—How, When, and Where to Sow Seeds.—Transplanting.—Packing of Vegetables for Shipping.—Preservation of Vegetables in Winter.—Insects.—Vegetables; their Variety and Cultivation.—Monthly Calendar of Operations.

Sent postpaid on receipt of $1.50.

PETER HENDERSON & CO.,
35 & 37 Cortlandt St., New York.

PRACTICAL FLORICULTURE.
BY
PETER HENDERSON.

The first edition was published in 1868, the second edition in 1873, and the third edition in December, 1878. It was written to teach how flowers and plants can best be "grown for profit." The success of this book has been fully as marked as that of "Gardening for Profit," when we consider that it only refers to a business exclusively a luxury. Upward of *thirty thousand* copies of this work have been sold, and it has been the means of establishing thousands of persons in an agreeable, and, in a majority of cases, profitable business. Its contents embrace:

Aspect and Soil.—Laying out the Lawn and Flower Garden.—Designs for Ornamental Grounds.—Planting of Flower Beds.—Soils for Potting.—Temperature and Moisture.—The Potting or Plants.—Cold Frames; Winter Protection.—Construction of Hot-beds.—Green-house Structures.—Green-houses attached to Dwellings.—Modes of Heating.—Base Burning Water Heater.—Propagation of Plants by Seeds.—What Varieties come True from Seed.—Propagation of Plants by Cuttings.—How Plants and Flowers are Grown.—Propagation of Lilies.—Culture of the Rose.—Culture of the Verbena.—Culture of the Tuberose.—Orchid Culture.—Holland Bulbs.—Cape Bulbs; Varieties and Culture.—Culture of Winter-Flowering Plants—Construction of Bouquets, Baskets, etc.—Wire Designs for Cut Flowers.—Hanging Baskets.—Parlor and Window Gardening.—Wardian Cases, Ferneries; etc.—Formation of Rockwork.—Insects.—Are Plants Injurious to Health?—Nature's Law of Colors.—Packing Plants.—Plants by Mail.—The Profits of Floriculture.—How to Become a Florist.—Short Descriptions of Soft-Wooded or Bedding Plants of the Leading Kinds.—What Flowers will Grow in the Shade.—Green-house and Stove or Hot-house Plants.—Annuals, Hardy Herbaceous, Perennial and Biennial Plants, Ornamental Shrubs and Climbers.—Culture of Grape Vines under Glass.—Diary of Operations for Each Day in the Year.

Sent postpaid on receipt of $1.50.

PETER HENDERSON & CO.,
35 & 37 Cortlandt St., New York.

GARDENING FOR PLEASURE.

BY

PETER HENDERSON.

This book was written by Mr. Henderson in 1875, to meet the wants of those desiring information on gardening for their private use, and who had no desire to make it a business. It is flattering to state that the demand for this book, for the time it has been issued, has been greater than either of its predecessors. Its scope of subjects is naturally greater than either "Gardening for Profit" or "Practical Floriculture," as it embraces directions for the propagation and culture of fruit, flowers, and vegetables. Its contents include:

Soil and Location.—Drainage.—Preparation of the Ground.—Walks.—Manures.—How to Use Concentrated Fertilizers.—Special Fertilizers for Particular Plants.—The Lawn.—Design for Garden.—Planting of Lawns and Flower Beds.—Fall or Holland Bulbs.—Propagation of Plants by Seeds.—Propagation of Plants by Cuttings.—Propagating by Layering.—About Grafting and Budding.—How Grafting and Budding are Done.—Treatment of Tropical Bulbs, Seeds, etc.—The Potting of Plants.—Winter-Flowering Plants.—Unhealthy Plants; the Remedy.—Plants Suited for Summer Decoration.—Hanging Baskets.—Window Gardening.—Parlor Gardening, or the Cultivation of Plants in Rooms.—Wardian Cases.—Ferneries.—Jardinieres.—Winter-Forcing the Lily of the Valley.—Green-houses attached to Dwellings.—A Detached Green-house or Grapery.—Heating by Hot Water.—Green-house Pits without Artificial Heat.—Combined Cellar and Green-house.—Hot-beds.—Shrubs.—Climbers and Trees.—Hardy Herbaceous Perennials.—Annual Flowering Plants.—Flowers which will Grow in the Shade.—Insects.—Mildew.—Frozen Plants.—Mulching.—Are Plants in Rooms Injurious to Health?—Shading.—The Laws of Color in Flowers.—Pruning.—Hardy Grapes.—Cold Grapery.—The Hot-house or Forcing Grapery.—The Strawberry.—Cottage Gardening; a Digression.—The Vegetable Garden.—Garden Implements.—Monthly Calendar of Operations.

Sent postpaid on receipt of $1.50.

PETER HENDERSON & CO.,

35 & 37 Cortlandt St., New York.

HENDERSON'S
HANDBOOK OF PLANTS.
BY
PETER HENDERSON.

This new work is designed to fill a want that many amateur and professional Horticulturists have often felt, the need of a concise yet comprehensive Dictionary of Plants. The work above named, written and compiled with great care, we think will fully meet such a want.

The scope of the work embraces the Botanical Name, Derivation, Linnæan and Natural Orders of Botany of all the Leading Genera of Ornamental and Useful Plants, up to the present time, (comprising every plant of importance relating to the mechanic arts, as well as to the green-house and vegetable garden,) with concise instructions for propagation and culture. A valuable feature of the book, particularly to amateurs, is the great care that has been given to obtain all known local or common names; and a comprehensive glossary of Botanical and Technical terms is also given, which will be found of great value even to the experienced Horticulturist.

As a book of reference, **HENDERSON'S HANDBOOK OF PLANTS** will take the place, for all practical purposes, of the expensive and voluminous European works of this kind, as it has been written with a view to meet the wants of those engaged in Horticulture in this country. Instructions for the culture of many important plants have been given at length.

HENDERSON'S HANDBOOK OF PLANTS is a large octavo volume of 412 pages, printed on fine white paper, and handsomely bound in cloth.

We will forward the book, postpaid by mail, on receipt of $3.00; or we will send it, as well as any or all of our other books, as a *Premium* on orders for *Seeds* or *Plants* selected from our Catalogue of "EVERYTHING FOR THE GARDEN." Full information as to how these Book Premiums may be obtained will be found in the Catalogue, which we shall be pleased to send to any address free of charge.

PETER HENDERSON & CO.,
35 & 37 Cortlandt St., New York.

www.ingramcontent.com/pod-product-compliance
Lightning Source LLC
Chambersburg PA
CBHW020805230426
43666CB00007B/869